Awakening The Actor Within

Awakening The Actor Within

A Twelve-Week Workbook To Recover
And Discover Your Acting Talents

C. Stephen Foster

Copyright © 2011 by C. Stephen Foster.

Library of Congress Control Number: 2011910352
ISBN: Hardcover   978-1-4628-9200-6
               Softcover   978-1-4628-9199-3
               Ebook   978-1-4628-9201-3

All rights reserved. No part of this book may be reproduced or transmitted in any form or by any means, electronic or mechanical, including photocopying, recording, or by any information storage and retrieval system, without permission in writing from the copyright owner.

This book was printed in the United States of America.

To order additional copies of this book, contact:
Xlibris Corporation
1-888-795-4274
www.Xlibris.com
Orders@Xlibris.com
98359

Contents

Introduction 17

"Awakening" 18
My Journey 20
So, What Is *Acting*, Really? 26
The Workbook 27
Waiting in the Wings 30
Basic Tools (Backstage) 34
Keep an Actor's Notebook 35
"I Remembers . . ." 35
Weekly Script Reading 36
Charting Your Progress 38
Acting Practice 38
Acting Practice Rules 41
Contract 43

Week 1
Act 1, Scene 1

Acting Is Healing 45
Let's Start at the Very Beginning 47
Don't Show Off, Show *Up!* 49
That's It! I Quit! 50
Canvas State 52
Scene Observation 53
"Off-Hollywood" 55
Panning for Gold 60

Tasks 64

1. Start an actor's notebook
2. "I remembers . . ."
3. Find a script and read it
4. Putting the light on it

5. Obtain a small houseplant
6. "Impersonations"

Week 1: Check-in 65

Week 2
Act 1, Scene 2

Who Are You? 66
"Self, Come In . . ." 67
"Terrible, Toos" 68
Inner Cast 69
Imagination 70
Willingness 72
Isolation 73
Accidents/Synchronicity/"Lights, Camera, Action" 76

Tasks 78

1. Who am I?
2. List five people who support your dreams
3. List ten things you could buy or do for your actor
4. List five people who are negative or destructive to your acting life
5. Buy new shoes
6. Movie madness: Select your favorite scene from your "vein of gold" list and get a copy of it (get ready to perform it!)
7. Describe ten accidents that have occurred in your life
8. Tell me about your "real" self
9. Make paper dolls from your "inner cast"
10. List ten roles you've already played in life

Week 2: Check-in 79

Week 3
Act 1, Scene 3

Toxic Block Syndrome 81
Suddenly, Become *Too* Busy 82
De Fence 83

What Are My Odds? 84
Learn from the Greats 85

Tasks 88

1. Perform your favorite scene from your "vein of gold" list
2. Give Oscar speech
3. How many hours this week did you spend practicing your acting?
4. List ten times when you've settled for less, slowed down, or stopped
5. List five different odd ball paths to approach your acting career
6. What do you bring to the part?
7. Name the suspects who stopped you from acting?
8. Find a biography or autobiography of someone *you* consider a *great* actor
9. Time travel: Write an "I remember . . ." from all your ages

Week 3: Check-in 90

Week 4
Act 1, Scene 4

The Hunger 91
Snakes "Hissing" in Your Garden 95
Patience and Waiting 96
Pop Quiz 99
Do One Thing Each Day for Your Actor 99
Don't Think 100
"I Want" Monologue 100

Tasks 101

1. Imagine how your favorite actor would play the role
2. What type are you? What type of characters are you drawn to?
3. Archive: Select a monologue that you used to love to perform
4. Catalog: Go back through your script reading and select a monologue and a scene
5. Go to an audition
6. Buy yourself some "audition" clothes

7. List five things that you place before your acting
8. Walking it out

Week 4: Check-in 103

Week 5
Act 2, Scene 1

The Script 105
Scene Exploration 106
Five Important Questions..106
Annie Hall—An Exercise 107
Putting "Actions" to Work in Your Scene Work 107
I Want..108
Assuming the Role...109
Character Study..110
Commitment to Character...111
Where Does the Character Live? 113
Observations 116
Audition Blues 116

Tasks 120

1. Where does the character live in you?
2. Examine your environment
3. Make a list of all the "methods" of acting you've tried
4. Character: How do you create a character?
5. Write an "I remember . . ."
6. "Circle game"
7. Perform a monologue from your "play reading"
8. Assemble a costume plot for your character
9. Go shopping for your character
10. Stay "in" and write an "I remember . . ." about five people you know
11. Go "out" and observe five people and write a character description
12. Actions: List twenty things you could do in your scene
13. When you read your next play, begin to jot down things the character's wants

Week 5: Check-in 121

Week 6
Act 2, Scene 2

"Money Makes the World Go Round!" 123
Danger! 126
Walking It Out...128
The Rejection Factor..129
Entrances...130
Character Soundtrack..131
Creating the *Right* Costume 132
Stop Dragging Your Feet..134

Tasks 134

1. Perform a scene from your "script reading"
2. Write an "I remember . . ." on how you made it
3. Create a soundtrack for your character
4. List all your artistic victories
5. Create a drag
6. My *greatest* moments
7. How many "nos" have you heard lately?
8. Write a monologue from your "I remembers . . ."
9. Write in your notebook five different entrances for one character

Week 6: Check-in 135

Week 7
Act 2, Scene 3

Acting Is "Action!"..136
Building the House 139
"Properties" of Acting...140
Scene from "I Remembers . . ." 142

Tasks 143

1. Perform your "I remember . . ." monologue
2. Dress up like a movie star
3. List all your artistic wounds
4. Write a scene from your "I remembers . . ."
5. Examine the environment in your scene
6. History of a props

Week 7: Check-in..143

Week 8
Act 2, Scene 4

Save the Drama for the Stage..144
Auditions Are Not Crisis...149
Quick Fix 152
I Booked It! 153
Some Roles I've Booked 154

Tasks 155

1. Reruns: My life on prime time! List ten positive things that have happened to you in your acting!
2. I booked it: List ten roles that you've booked (or ten jobs you've landed)
3. Buried treasure: List ten dreams or projects that you've given up on!
4. Create a new you from the *old* you
5. List ten roles that you want to play
6. Perform your "I remember . . ." scene

Week 8: Check-in..157

Week 9
Act 3, Scene 1

Where Is My Career?..158
Attention! Target Shoppers! Creating Your Package 160
"Attention: Casting! *You!*"..162

Tasks 163

1. Create a logline for your talent in the third person
2. List your faults or honor your faults
3. My "star" self
4. Headshot or resume inventory: Who do you see in your picture? What does your resume say about you?
5. Picture morgue
6. Career map
7. Age appropriate
8. List ten things you don't like about yourself. How can they serve you as an actor?

Week 9: Check-in..164

Week 10
Act 3, Scene 2

Public and Private Self..165
Don't Engage 166
Battle vs. Game...170

Tasks 174

1. Them vs. Me
2. Florence Nightingale: List ten needy people, places, and things that distract you from your path
3. List ten people who you think have it "going on!"
4. Change of scenery: Change your "look"
5. Public and private self
6. Life game

Week 10: Check-in..175

Week 11
Act 3, Scene 3

Natural Talent vs. Trained Talent 176
Using the Day Gig Blues 182
When to Stop Paying Dues 184

Reviews and Agents 186

Tasks 187

1. "But what I really want to do is act, but what I do is . . ."
2. Daily inventory
3. My dream agent
4. My tools
5. What I need?
6. Ask for help
7. Reviews

Week 11: Check-in 188

Week 12
Act 3, Scene 4

Trust the "Process" 189
The Eye of the Tiger 191
Flipping the Switch (I See Dead People!) 193
"Acting Is Interacting" 195

Tasks 197

1. List five people on "the other side" who you can ask for help
2. Write short paragraphs of why you still want to act
3. Counting courage: Write a short list of things that give you courage
4. Call your "acting buddy" and create a three-month "action plan" and check in once a week on your progress
5. Make a quick list of your current fears and angers in your notebook about your continued acting career
6. Continued commitment
7. Share this book

Week 12: Check-in 198

This workbook is dedicated to Chuck Pelletier,
who always encourages me to reach for the stars.

Acknowledgments

I'd like to thank the following for their help and guidance in putting this book together:

My great-grandmother, Granny, for giving me the model of creativity.

My family for nurturing and supporting my crazy life path.

Chuck Pelletier who always believed there was more to me than meets the eye. Joseph O'Donnell for having the courage to cast me in *Off Hollywood* when others were saying "*no!*" and for knowing what to do with my talent. Mace Lombardo and Suzanne Stokes for being the most sensational costars ever. To everyone connected with the movie *Off Hollywood*, put your name here: _____. Thank you.

My early tribe: Joel Craig and Chris Reidy, thank you for giving me a platform to express myself, and to Scott Wilkerson for showing me "*how*" to use my gifts.

My "Hollywood" pals—Julie Sheppard, Nomi Lyonns, Amy Penney, and Jeff Copeland—thank you for being in my corner no matter what trials I faced.

My fellow writer Paula Sanders for encouraging me to finish writing the workbook by telling me how much her acting students benefited from it.

My teachers and mentors: Jeff Paul, Stacy Schronk, Norval Sykes, and all the ones in books that I have not met.

My acting students who taught me along the way and helped me refine these tools and principles, and Carol Brook for believing in them from day one.

All my friends and fans in Facebook land, thanks for sharing your stories with me.

And to you; put your name here_____!

Introduction

My name is C. Stephen Foster, and I am an actor and writer. I write and act in films, TV, stage, webisodes, or any other medium created. My journey has not been a pleasure cruise with velvet curtain calls. It's been rewarding, yes, but it's been hard work. Everything about my life is about acting and writing. As the years go forward, I do more and more acting and writing. All my lessons in life come from my moving between the page and the performance. These two art forms have forged me, molded me, and sometimes deflated me, but have also brought great joy and rewards. I'm writing this book to those hopeful, eager actors who want to try their talents and put them into the world! I hope the advice you get here is clear, specific, and helpful. I do want to remind you before you dive in that *you* are on your own course. This book deals with the adventures of acting and keeping on when the easiest thing to do is to quit.

I have had years of grandeur and years of failure, I've worked hard, I've written scripts that have been produced, I've been in many, many shows from flop to feature films, and I can honestly say to you, if you stick to this journey, you will be rewarded someday! That's the hopeful part, but I want to warn you, it's a hard life to live! You will be asked to sacrifice everything for it, but if you want to give all, you'll be rewarded. You may not become the next Brad Pitt, but you may have a body of work that is as strong as his abs in *Thelma and Louise*. Did I mention I'm a comedian? Sometimes, I'll crack a joke in these pages to lessen the tension. Acting and writing can be a very daunting subject.

> *We are shaped and fashioned by what we love.*
> —Goethe

The workbook you are holding is about taking a journey, a voyage into the world known as "acting." Some of you may be "acting" actors, some of you might have started good and then quit, some of you will be eager to start, some of you might be afraid to try, while others might need a refresher course or a jump start back into it. Some of you are probably coming to this teaching discouraged, dismayed, while others might be already far along the way; it doesn't matter. These pages are the culmination of over fifteen years of work as an actor and a teacher, and I've seen many students succeeding with these tools. Use this workbook to benefit *you*. Wherever you start is a good place.

This workbook might not strike you at first as having anything to do with *real* acting, but the tools laid out in the following pages have *everything* to do with acting. Acting can't be defined in simple terms, nor can it be taught in a linear method. I've learned by doing.

You will find a lot of tools to use to build yourself up. Some will work for you and others won't. I suggest you try them all and then decide later if one isn't right for you. Acting is willy-nilly and is as individual as each actor who has ever lived or who will ever live. The journey you are about to embark upon are some of my ideas, philosophies, and tools that have "worked" for me and my students. They are active tools. The more you use them, the better they will work for you. I hope they serve you well. The path or journey you are about to engage in is and should be fun. I hope to get you "addicted" to acting and writing. The more you do it, the less unhappy you are. Acting is actually very healing. Acting is therapy—a healing energy lies in acting.

This workbook will help you recover and discover your acting abilities. This is neither a "get rich quick" book nor a "break into Hollywood in five easy steps" book. This is a workbook concerning recovering from our acting "blocks" and rebuilding confidence and taking our power back as actors.

"Awakening"

What is "awakening"? It's becoming aware that you really desire to act. It has to do with admitting that we are "blocked" as actors and that we need help. Coming to terms that we've settled for limits, have settled into lives that don't really fit our needs, or accepted vocations for the benefit of others while our dreams drift somewhere in our minds. It's about learning that the universe actually wants us to act. We come into our own gifts and let other powers work through us. We awake on two levels—the first level has to do with admitting where we've misplaced and misspent our energies, where we've not taken ourselves seriously. The second level involves the power in which to use those talents. The direction we choose to travel. We awaken to our heart's desire. We begin to glow with that fire we thought was snuffed out (by others or ourselves).

What I'm talking about by the term or word "blocked" is a standstill of energy—a misplacement or stagnation of energy. "Blocked" means that we feel vexed, frustrated, angry, and unable to "make it" as actors. Through this course, we will begin to remove these inner barriers, and our natural talent, which is always just beneath our consciousness, will begin flowing. Unblocking our acting means we shift our energies, we remove the obstructions, and we trudge ahead and then outward events align with our internal shifts.

What we begin to learn when we begin to "awaken" our actor is that the gift has been with us forever, and we can develop them. This takes courage and practice. We have this belief that we walk out on the stage or in front of the camera and we're perfect. Expecting this perfection is dangerous. Practice makes perfect. Practice is the cure for depression, for feeling empty and listless. When we begin to practice, we are developing muscles. We are changing how we approach our acting. We are not changing our goals. We are not settling for less than, sloppy or unfocused acting. We are, however, building slowly. We are learning how to trust our instinctive talents. Some of us may have never acknowledged the fact that we really desire to act more than anything else. Or we may have stopped due to the circumstances of our lives. It seldom has to do with "talent" but the accurate organization and use of that talent.

I urge you to go slowly with yourself as you recover and discover your actor. Going through my things today (throwing the old out so the new could come in), I found award nomination certificates from high school. I had almost forgotten that hard work, the feeling of accomplishment when I won the White Flower Award—the award given to the most well-rounded theater student. I feel sort of sad looking back because I began so great and then got discouraged. I sat on my floor knowing that I had made some wrong choices, but how could they be wrong because they had led me here?

I'm writing this book for those of you who might have no hope. I'm writing this book in the hopes that today you will start. I'm writing this book for the ones who dream. I'm writing this book in the hopes that those who are lost will find their way. I'm writing this so the broken can be healed. I'm writing this book for future actors to come and to make a hard journey less lonely. I'm writing this book so those discouraged, dissatisfied, and dismayed will find a new way.

This book is about reconnecting to the true self, connecting to what truly makes us happy. It's my belief and experience that acting makes me happy, whole and complete. We will step by step build a sense of strength. We will also learn how to risk a week at a time.

I can never, never teach you *how* to act. I can only give you suggestions. Acting is a process, a journey that has to be traveled, acting is a personal process. There are many forms and schools of acting.

Because you are yourself (just as you already are), a truly, talented, original entity waiting, wishing to act, you need only believe in it, trust it and *use* it. Your creativity has a magic quality that is unique unto you. No two actors are the same just like no two blades of grass are the same.

As a young actor, I was trained to listen to others about my craft, not myself. This is the big lesson: the first voice you should listen to when attempting to act is your own. You own your work. You are the one onstage, on-screen on TV. We forget this so easily.

Nothing can teach you to act like acting.
—Bette Davis

My Journey

How and why did I come to write this book about acting? This is a part of my journey.

I was a very shy boy growing up. I was born and raised in Texas, and I remember getting my first laugh in third grade. It thrilled and excited me unlike anything I've ever felt. I played a noun and pushed the guy standing next to me playing a verb, and the class went wild. That summer, I saw the movie *Grease,* and I was captivated. I wanted to find a way to make it into a stage play (I didn't know it came from a play!), so I corralled all my friends into doing a production in the backyard. I remember building a fun house in the back of a garage. As the years went by, I wrote little shows and cast my sister in them, but I still didn't think acting was anything I could do. Skip then to high school . . . My career began by some miracle. In ninth grade, we got to choose our electives for the upcoming year. On the list were woodshop, home economics, gymnastics, and auto repair. I saw on the list "stagecraft," and a little voice said, "Take that!" and I signed on.

So, in high school, I became more interested in drama classes than any other subject. I even won an award for my efforts, but then college is where I got blocked and I stopped. I want to begin where the blocking began for me and how I started again. You might relate to my story or some part of it. I was young, bright-eyed in college, wanting to take on my acting and take the world by storm. I was green, naive, and thought I knew everything. I had my hand in all of the pies in the theater department. When I wasn't in a play, I was working on a scene or doing props, stage management. I took theater classes exclusively because I was starting to express myself. I was walking down a hall one day after school with a load of books weighing me down, and I passed by a teacher's office. She asked me if I was auditioning for the play *Romeo and Juliet*.

"Na," I responded in my southern drawl.

To which she responded, "Why not?"

And I said, "There's no part for me."

She said, "You don't know that! It's a huge cast and you should audition!"

I personally like to think of her as one of my guides. (I've had a series of these wise people on earth who encouraged and inspired me.)

I showed up at the audition with a piece from *Macbeth* that I had memorized in high school English class. Well, midway through my "Tomorrow and Tomorrow" speech, I forgot my lines cold and the director actually fed me my lines and after the audition he told me to come back the next day after looking at the role of Peter, the nurse's servant. I immediately ran to the library and grabbed a copy and studied the role, still not expecting anything. Well, miraculously, I got the role!

I recall now that play yielded me my first comedic spot, my first good review ("an interesting character is Peter . . ."), and my first paying role in a murder mystery show. I was ready to open on Broadway. I wish I had taken those experiences and gone on to act in other plays in Los Angeles, but what happened next is the point of the story and probably the point of the book. I got bitten by discouragement.

The next semester, it was announced they were doing *One Flew over the Cuckoo's Nest,* and I knew I had to have the part of Billy Bibbit or simply die. So I spent the summer staying out of the sun and reading the script and book. After all, it was the same director who did *Romeo and Juliet,* and I had done such a great job in that show. He had to pick me! I was perfect for that role. The big audition came, and when the call sheet came out, the entire play was cast (with all my friends) except for Billy Bibbit! What was the problem? It had to be me! And then a few more days went by and a name I didn't recognize was on the list. He cast a beginning acting student to play *my* part. I was mortified, ashamed, and crushed. How could this happen to me? I had a mentor who was directing me in a performance art piece at the time told me, "Stephen, I'd go out and audition for other parts." Looking back, it's some of the best advice I've ever been given. But I didn't take his advice. With a heart of lead, I took the director's consolation prize of being his "assistant" instead of acting. *Ouch!* I sat through rehearsal after rehearsal, taking notes, gathering props, and typing to-do lists, and I was truly what Julia Cameron calls a "shadow artist." (An artist who hides in the shadows of declared artists and works close to the art form, but not the read deal.) I even gave the actor who was playing Billy acting tips on how to improve his performance. (Notes I had taken when I was preparing for the role!) This "behind the scenes" work never carried me closer to the stage.

I kept trying to play in a field where it was obvious I would not get cast. I continued to show up for class work, but I hated the fact that this *one* director (the giant guru of the faculty) wouldn't cast me. I remember at one point, I was his "assistant" again (who ever said I was a fast learner?) for some high bow Pinter thing he was doing, and he was having casting troubles with an actor when he looked at me and said, casually like flipping a cigarette ash into the can, "If you were a foot taller, I'd cast you!" If I had the gumption I have today, I would have told him where and how to get off. But I held it in and buried it beneath the surface. I cringe remembering now as to how vulnerable and wanting of his approval I was. I was such a goody-goody actor. "If I'm good enough, and do what they want, they will cast me (I hope . . .)," my philosophy went. Some jacked up theory we're taught to please people. At that same college, I played a corpse (in drag!) in a production for the artist-director who later didn't cast me as well.

Add to the above story, my parents' disapproval of my career choice, and is it any wonder I stopped acting? For three years! The household

I grew up in was *not* of the determined ilk. If something was difficult, challenging, or discouraging, it was easier to quit than to keep right on, and then you could sit in a world of "they are just against me" instead of pushing for what you want. Ever stop doing something you love? Cold turkey? It hurts like hell. I remember thinking, "Well, if I can't act, I'll write! I'll write plays and put my friends in them." It had been my habit to read as many plays as possible when I was learning to act (something I still do). So I wrote my first play—I jumped into it like a fish to water. I wrote it for two friends of mine. I'm lucky (in hindsight) that I had writing to fall back on. Writing kept me afloat and eventually led me back to the path of acting.

The beginning of my real lessons in acting began when I stopped acting. Not doing acting was the most difficult time of my life. I had started of with lots of talent and enthusiasm and then I got discouraged. I didn't come from a family that supported me, and when I got shot down, I didn't have a mentor to help coach me. I didn't know how to take my raw talent and turn it into ways I could get cast. I was one of those actors that didn't fit a specific bill, so I got shuffled off to the sidelines. "Lots of energy, lots of talent, but we just can't use him."

This created a lot of conflict within my head concerning acting. I also wanted so badly to please, to make the teachers and peers like me. And I remember reaping wound after wound of doing "service" of backstage work—I heard this was "paying your dues." This angle never worked because when it came time to cast a show, the directors knew I could do lights, costumes, or props, and I wouldn't get in the show, but close to it. I remember also giving actors lessons during this time (teaching has always been one of my "hidden" talents). But my real talent was being on the stage, making people laugh.

I had to "give up" my acting in order to learn how much I loved it. I wasn't one of the lucky ones who had my talent fall into gracious hands or fertile ground. The first thing I had to learn was to not put my creativity into *anyone's* hands. It was mine. I owned it. It was my responsibility to recover my talent and do something with it. When I decided to act again, I decided that I would never lie and say I will do other tasks in the theater except act or write (of course, the shows I'd write would be for me!), and I've kept that promise. My life became about acting and writing and using those two basic tools to stay unblocked. And in doing so, I had to learn some tools to create. I also had to discard some of the rubbish I was taught both in my family (who knew nothing about the business) and from society (where *everyone* seems to know about the business).

Several months later, a friend decided to put together a writing group, and it was at this group where I met through a book my first in a series of healers or teachers. The title of the book was *Writing Down the Bones* by Natalie Goldberg, and her work crossed my path like a lightening bolt. I had never been encouraged to write, to write about who I am. I learned how to trust my own mind and my own process. It was so simple: "Keep your hand moving," and I did. That book was branded on my mind like a tattoo. So I wrote. I filled journal after journal until I wrote poems, plays, reviews, and short stories while my acting ambitions lay dormant.

I didn't know it at the time, but I was being given the keys to a whole new kingdom. Later, when I was thinking about how to do acting, I borrowed her gentle but firm insistence and came up with the term "acting practice." The simple idea that we can act without a "middleman" or "guru" and build things on our own excited me.

I became a poet and journalist using that book. Then as fate would dictate, I lived with a very blocked actor who kept telling me he wanted to act, but . . . , and I remember I gave him a book called *Setting Free the Actor* by Ann Brebner, which I should have given to myself. What do they say in twelve-step groups? "If you have one finger pointing at someone else, you have three pointing back at yourself?" Well, I believe it cuts both ways: If you're pointing at someone saying "they have talent, they are so gifted, and they are funny," that's a *big* clue as to what *you* want. I recall telling him, "You're a brilliant actor, just trust yourself," and I would have gotten much further to tell myself that.

So I kept writing. Fast-forward the movie four years later. Somebody handed me a copy of *The Artist's Way* by Julia Cameron, and I began to unblock my creativity, but still not admitting my acting dreams. I was stuck in a dead-end trap of a job at a record store. I *hated* it. The manager doesn't like my little Bette Midler's "Sophie Tucker" jokes and Judy Garland and Liza Minnelli impersonations. He thought I should put CDs away. I didn't have the heart to tell him that I was working on my brilliance and he should shove off. I wasn't a loud mouth then; I took it as a personal attack, but I kept doing it in spite of his bad attitude. I was a writer at that point, and I was publishing poetry and writing reviews. Acting was as far away from me as I was from it. I never dreamed I would act again.

Enter a striking young man straight off the bus from the Deep South with piercing blue eyes, who takes a liking to my little sense of humor and my eclectic personality. And we began to "play" together and do improvisation while we worked, and we decided to do a performance party at our house, which eventually turned into the first show I did called *Divanalysis*. This show was my resurrection and my salvation. I was finally shown and guided to my true acting ambition. I was to write and to act together and create my own breaks.

I wasn't given that option in high school or college. I was a little miffed that nobody had told me such practical advice that I'm giving you. Keep at it! Keep going until you get there, and don't be mean to yourself! God only knows there are a lot of people out there who will be mean to you! It took me a long time and many years of beating myself up until I discovered to be nice to my actor, to be sweet him. That's the great "secret" that they don't teach in school or life. Remember, in the film and TV series *Fame,* when they have the teacher screaming at the students, "You want *fame*, baby? *This* is *where* you *pay!*" I think teachers like that need to be tarred and feathered. Without ego strength, some actor will perish in such hostile environments. I did!

> *There is someone in the audience tonight who auditioned me 30 years ago, and told me I was untalented and unphotogenic and I should quit trying to be an actress. Well, 30 years later, here I am, Emmy in hand. I won't mention your name. But you know who you are. And you WILL be in The Book!*
>
> —Rue McClanahan (Emmy Acceptance Speech)

I also remember as a young actor how I used to play "their" game and not mine. I always compared myself to other actors and felt that what they did was the true or *"real"* way to act, although it never worked for me. It didn't feel right. Somewhere along the path we believe we have to "prove" ourselves or "pay our dues" to them in duty and service and that's how acting becomes laborious and difficult. We have a mythology that we must please and appease "them" and maybe someday (if we're good and lucky) they will recognize our talents and give us our big break. The goody two-shoes approach never worked for me. I've always found that I have associated with the underdog who rises up against the odds. I believe in Carol Burnett's philosophy: "Make your own breaks."

"Make your own breaks" breaks us from the habit and thinking that somebody outside of us tells us what and how we are to act. It means that we take responsibility. We do our work each day and what we desire will come when it needs to. When Ruth Gordon (who had a long, long, long career) couldn't get cast in theater or movies, she wrote . . . she wrote plays for herself and then screenplays with her husband Garson Kanin. I have done the same thing and encourage actors to write and develop projects for themselves, and someday, someone will write parts for *you!*

I had to change my entire approach to acting. I knew there had to be another angle to the way acting was taught. I knew there were many outdated, outmoded, and overused methods that didn't serve a lot people. There simply had to be another solution, or maybe a piece to the puzzle that wasn't being explained to people. In short, a different path in which actors could safely walk. How did I come up with these new expressions? I lived them. I walked them. I made them up to dig myself out of my own pit. They became the games I played when I needed courage to go on.

My quest and question became: How do I keep functioning as an actor amid the disappointments, the heartaches, the flops, the "nos," and even my own ego trips at times? I just keep moving. That's what I learned through acting. Through it all you keep acting, trial and error. Mistakes only lead to further insights and explorations to larger risks.

Genius is 1% inspiration and 99% perspiration.
—Thomas Edison

So, What Is *Acting*, Really?

I had to dismantle the old, toxic ideas (myths) we have about acting—acting as told to us by teachers, gurus, family, and society. I had to drop the guru, the method, and the technique, basically, the idea that we need other people to show us or tell us *how* to act. I'm not saying actors should stop going to classes and learning, but I believe we know more than we allow ourselves to know. We can learn by doing instead of the old-fashioned way: you prepare a scene or monologue and you put it up before the teacher (or great, powerful casting directors), who then criticizes all you've done. I believe this creates shame and diminishes the spirit of the poor actor who has put effort and love into his creation. It's not applauded for the attempt (process) but criticized and overly attacked as if it were a polished performance (product). The greatest directors I've worked with are the ones who take what I offer, trim the fat off it, and leave me alone. I don't do my best acting when I get in my head.

"I hate criticism!" Ruth Gordon said. Because she knew that *she* knew best. I believe we should all take this protective angle to our acting. The challenge is to believe in *yourself* and your talent. We need to find our actor and help his spirit grow.

> *The whole idea of creation is mysterious and wonderful,*
> *it's a bottomless craft, which is why I love it so much.*
> —Uta Hagen

The Workbook

What we will be doing over the next twelve weeks is altering the trajectory of our lives and our careers as actors. We will be gravitating toward our goals and authentic acting talents one step, one day at a time. We will recover our actor and create some tools to keep us acting so we hopefully won't quit again. We will learn how to save the drama for our creativity and *use* it for acting material. We will gradually repair our acting careers and have more freedom in our lives. We will be giving ourselves a creative "makeover." We will act our way into writing and write our way into acting.

I'll be your guide. I'll be guiding you along your own acting path. I want to be clear about this: we are each unique and powerful, and our paths are diverse. Your path is your own, not mine. You own it, you walk it. What you feel, think, and create in the course of this work is of vital importance. I cannot wave a magic wand over your head and say, "Poof, you are now an actor!" I wish I could make it that simple. But when dealing with acting blocks, we are dealing with long forgotten memories and fragile emotions. These dreams, desires, and impulses do not die hard, they die painfully. And recovering them might involve a few tears and bouts of anger. We will learn to convert those old fears and doubts into courage and faith. When we don't act, we die a little. "Everyday, a little death." The song by Sondheim goes. How true. And every day that we don't act, we feel a little more "off." Through the tools in this book, we are going to get you "on" again.

The workbook is laid out in a three-act screenplay structure (beginning, middle, and end). Each week covers a specific area that we will work through. The first four weeks deal with the basic acting blocks and graining our footing to try again. Weeks 5-8 concentrate on scripts and characters. The final four weeks focus on the career aspects (marketing yourself).

Each week, you will be given essays to read and tasks to accomplish (in addition to your daily writing and weekly script reading), and each week, you will be asked to "check-in," this is to map your progress, not to criticize yourself. You'll have to give yourself some creative time to read the chapters and do the "homework." My suggestion is: work through the entire book completely once. If you only do *one* task in a given week, that is enough. Do your check-in and go on to the next chapter until you've completed the twelve weeks. You can always circle back and do the tasks that you've missed.

I do know this: whatever "comes up" to block you in this book is the exact same thing that blocks you as an actor. (Some of the common ones are: money, time, not enough support, bad relationships, toxic sex, alcohol, and drugs.) When one of these clever little critters leaps up to sabotage you, celebrate because you are seeing a pattern that you are working on breaking. Once you see and recognize the "blocks," you can begin to create healthier ways to deal with your fears and angers.

Once you begin to unblock using the methods outlined in these chapters, you will experience a breakthrough. You will recover and discover your actor and learn ways to handle sabotage and fear. I have watched the miracles of actor's recovery over and over again as I have taught both publicly and privately. I have seen shy and timid students take center stage after years of hiding their talents. (I include myself in this category.) One of my students, Julie, said, "I feel like I've been saving it up and now I'm ready to share it with the world!"

When we begin to ask for help and work on our acting, the help shows up. I don't ask you to believe any of this. Just experiment with the tools in the book and watch how quickly things start to click for you.

This workbook is about taking notice of what is ours, naming and claiming it, and then *using* it. This can be challenging and even frustrating in a world full of naysayers. "What's a naysayer?" you may ask. A "naysayer" is anyone who tells us we can't or we shouldn't. You know those people, places, and things that deaden our spirits and douse the fire of our dreams. These people often reveal themselves as our teachers, family, jealous, blocked friends, agents, coworkers, and even ourselves at times. It's anyone who says *"no"* in any fashion to our dreams. You might want to keep it a secret that you are undergoing this process until you gain some momentum. Nothing can make you "block" faster than telling a well-meaning but negative friend your intentions.

I wish this book to be a bridge for you, a way for you to cross back over to using your god-given acting talents while also forging your authentic talents. This book will also use the terms "God," "universe," and "spirit." Please don't freak out. I use the terms only to speak of the "nonphysical" elements that we tap into when we are fully engaged in our acting "process." So, when I speak of God in these pages, don't go insane on me. Just try using some of the tools to see if those "invisible" elements start to help you.

It's all in the game and the way you play it!
—Judy Garland

What we will be engaging in with these acting tools is a series of "games." As children we used to play games, but we forget how to play them because we become adult and lost our ability to use our imaginations. Acting is no more than playing games. Let yourself play with these tools. This is an experimental process. When I'm lighthearted about my acting, I'm usually free and having a ball and enjoy my life, but when I think of it merely as a career, I'm stymied and worried about what "they" (the Big Kids) will think and say about my acting. What I'm suggesting is we do let ourselves act daily and worry about the outcome later. Marianne Williamson who taught "The Course in Miracles" tells us, "If you were meant to be a singer, then why on earth would God want you to do accounting?"

Acting is not a chore. Acting is a gift, and it's our responsibility to use it. I think we make acting so hard we forget delight, passion, and love.

It's my goal to train you, who want to act to forget the odds, to act all the time. The moment you put your hand in, you are turning the odds in your favor. Acting does not have to be so heavy—so draped in seriousness. I think when approached from a stance of love we get more mileage, but we are used to making it our "work." Viewed this way, we are robbing ourselves from the joy of doing it. We keep waiting for our turn. This is a crime to our creative child. Everything we do in our career should be viewed as a potential of having a ball. We get further along if we play as opposed to *work*.

Waiting in the Wings

When I hear blocked actors talk about their acting ("I tried acting, but I gave it up . . ."), I can feel the years of remorse. I can hear all the energy escape them and then I hear the excuses. I hear, "Well, you see . . . ," and I listen at how many ways we have at getting out of using our gifts. We have a lot of "baggage" around what being an actor means. We have got it fixed in our minds that there are only a few "lucky" actors and the rest of us are like old milk that settles to the bottom of the pail. And we do grow pale and we do settle, but our souls still long for expression.

We get the high-paying job. We are so used to doing what others have prescribed for us, so we settle—we settle back and we settle down. We settle for less when we know deep down what would make us happy, joyous, and free. Each of us is an interesting, unique person struggling to be born. What we don't often admit is how much we would love to act. Or we admit it and then immediately discount it. "I would, but . . ." the story goes. I think what we are desperately missing is support around our desires. We are surrounded by supporters who think we should settle down for our own good. I say go all the way. Life was meant to be lived! Burn the fire you were given because that is when you are truest when you are fully alive. That is why we don't risk or reach for more. We grow accustomed to "no" and letting the "no" stop and hinder us. Instead, say "yes." And take an action toward your acting, and if one action or audition doesn't do it, take two or three or however many it takes. I'm not only talking about willpower, but I'm talking more about the willingness to show up for the action. If you are in the action, you don't have time to weep and moan about the awful breaks because you are in the game!

We have bought into the psychology of society that tells us: "there is no money, you're not the right type, or you have to know the right contacts, etc." and when we hear "no," we lose heart. There are other ways we get blocked: we get overly criticized by the acting teacher who hasn't set foot on a stage in over twenty years or casting directors who have never acted or worse friends who are afraid to act. The blocks can also be "business" related: our agent drops us, the film goes over budget, the play we're in gets lousy reviews, a creative partner turns "sour" on us. So we stop.

We settle back and we settle down saying, "One day . . . ," and we play this game until we believe it's "too late." But I never believe in time or age. We also think we have to "make it" by the time we are twenty; otherwise, we paint ourselves as failures. We forget that acting is a huge learning process with lessons always to be learned. We can learn lessons about business, we can learn lessons of networking, and we can learn lesson about saying "no." We forget that we must continually focus on what we still have to work on. The trail is ahead of us, not behind us.

In short, there is a lot of pain around our acting careers. We often don't flag and mourn our losses. We say, "Oh, who am I kidding anyway . . . What did you expect? It's all a racket anyway!" And we stay in the endless job we loathe because our enthusiasm has diminished. We wait tables, work in tireless offices, or do lights, costumes, or props instead of trying to act. We hope and pray that maybe someone will recognize us and throw us into the spotlight. We wait in the wings praying for a miracle instead of taking that leap onto the stage. But how can we take that leap when our legs are broken or we don't have enough support?

Now, let me be clear, props, costumes, makeup, and sets are all fine and great occupations (just like waiting tables, office work . . .) if your heart is in it or if you need the cash (but remember, *you're an actor first!*). If you're good at costumes, then do costumes, but if inside you are secretly wishing, hoping to act, well, I say start *now,* today.

That's what we'll be doing in this workshop. We will learn to take tiny baby steps and make notes on our progress. I urge you to trust your process and let go of the product. Let go of the drama or trauma of acting and *feel* your way back into encouragement, hope, and inspiration. Let yourself "feel" this process, not "think" it. Being too "intelligent" can cripple a recovering creative artist.

These tools are used to build confidence, to teach you to think and act for yourself. These little games we play will remold your career. I ask you not to believe me, but to try them and see what happens. If you let yourself, you'll be surprised at how quickly it works. I'm not promising overnight stardom, but you'll certainly begin to *feel* like a star and thus you'll be on your way!

I encourage you to build a foundation for yourself, a fortress—a place of safety where you're less afraid to act and freer to create. Together we'll create solid foundation, and I'll give you tools to build an acting house. Some of these tools might make you wince. Remember, your inner skeptic and rebel is out to undermine you. Don't be fooled. Growing hurts.

It has been fun for me to watch students examine and explore their lives and turn them around into creative careers.

> *Creativity is a blend of masculine and feminine energies.*
> *It's the receiving of that creative force (Feminine)*
> *and the expression of it (Masculine).*
> —Shakti Gawain

During my career, I've had to pick myself up, pick up the pieces, and get back up on the horse. I've learned to act whether I "feel" like it or not. I recently heard that jockeys are considered some of the strongest athletes. I know one of the hardest things to do is "get down" to our acting. There are so many good excuses but never enough reasons. We want to wait until we are in the right mood, until we are fixed or healed enough. But you'll soon discover that as you recover your acting potential, it's actually more painful not to act. One simple question you might ask yourself is, "Did I work on my acting today?" If you answer is "yes," then give yourself some applause, and if "no" rings in your head, try again tomorrow. Always be gentle with your actor.

The very first thing I'm going to say is this: You have to take action. In order to learn how to act, you have to do the "play." The quicker you get started and stay started, the faster you will advance. The point is to stay started. Stay a beginner. There is tremendous energy in being a beginner. There are nerves, fears, and eagerness. Use those energies. I've done my best work when I've had no logical idea of what I was doing, but I felt alive! When I felt like I was out on a limb and was taking a risk.

Stay Hungry. Stay Foolish. And I have always wished that for myself. And now, as you graduate to begin anew, I wish that for you.
—Steve Jobs

We think about doing, but we put every excuse in our way. We know we are brilliant, talented—we know deep within this is true, yet we forget it quickly when adversity strikes. We spend and squander our time, money, and lives on the things that take us away from the impulse to act. Instead of letting acting be our habit, we let everything else have our attention and priority. Why do we do this? We do this because we are afraid. We put it down because we are fearful of our own incredible, unique powers.

It's been my woeful experience to notice that I'll put my attention on anything besides my desire to act. I'll put my attention on the drama of the day job or the lack of money instead of asking the question, "Did I work on my acting today?" Instead of doing the job to serve our careers as an actor, we'll work very hard at somebody's business (and even do overtime!), yet we seldom do the service for ourselves. We are afraid what will happen if we get selfish, self-centered, and do what we love. We are fearful of how it will look to "them." We don't think of our careers as a business. We believe acting has to be done around the edges. Like the faint rainbow in the distance, we are always one step behind.

We make speeches to ourselves and others: "I could be on a sitcom! I should be on Broadway . . . ," yet we don't put the hours into it. We don't give it our *full* 100 percent attention. We hope and pray one day some magic person will wave a magic wand, hand us the golden keys to the kingdom, and make us (motivate us) pursue our dreams. We must always have our oar in the water (no matter what the sea "looks" like), our ears pricked for our advancement. So let's get started. Let's not waste time as we have miles to go together.

It is not my point to discount, discredit, or diminish the great acting teachers and philosophers or gurus even, but to give hope and help to those who need attention and healing, to help guide actors who have lost their way, and to put people back onto the road they stopped going down because of old abuse and unacknowledged pain. Once we begin to examine what holds us back, they begin to lose their powers over us, and we begin to slowly gain in strength. Muscles are not built in a day, and your recovery and discovery won't happen in a day, a month, or even a year (although great strides will be made if you just keep traveling.)

I think it would be interesting to go back to high school and see how many people who wanted so desperately to act and see how many actually are.

Basic Tools (Backstage)

In my workshops, I encourage students to act and write and not divide the two—it's part of the actor's mythology that actors are dumb (powerless). Not true. Directors want to work with smart, imaginative actors. Writing is the "ground" for my acting. I take many, many notes before, during, and after I act. (In fact, I hope one day to publish all my journals so other actors can see *how* I've worked.) Acting is an "outward" process; writing is an "inward" process. Writing helps me to create character bits. I usually write out character bits while I'm going over the script looking for clues. Actors should write; writers should act. The more you do both, the better you get at both. When I'm not officially acting in a play or movie, I read scripts and write plays and screenplays. Writing sharpens my acting and acting sharpens my writing. I've become adept at both and can now do each with skill and ease. I don't do a lot of talking about the two because I am busy doing. It is my hope that you do the same. I hear actors tell me all the time, "I can't write." Then I have them engage in "I remembers . . ." and all of a sudden, they find they do write very well.

The following are the elementary tools that my students have used over the years.

Keep an Actor's Notebook

Think of this as your cookbook. You will write out the tasks in the course (and weekly check-ins) put recipes of characters, "I remembers . . ." and plots for your career, and write about your auditions (the good, the bad, and the indifferent). I keep a notebook for each character I do. I call them as "character maps." At the end of twelve-week course, you'll be able to witness for yourself you own remarkable progress. I usually buy an old (and inexpensive) spiral notebook and collage the cover with actual pictures of myself and the dreams I'm trying to accomplish. Think fun! Think big and childish. Not school or college. This is your own special "dream" book to be used during this course. Let that be your first "*action!*"

"I Remembers . . ."

The first tool, I'd like to suggest is daily writing. I call it "nonsense memory" or "I remembers . . ." This is a daily stream of images or bits of your life that you'll put down on the page. Find time each day and begin with the sentence "I remember . . ." and write a full page. When you get stuck, go back to the sentence "I remember . . . ," and keep writing. Keep these in your notebook. I suggest you don't read them for a while. I ask you to do this to build your stamina to dig into your own mind for images. When you're writing your "I remembers . . . ," you're trying to tap into the ground of your life and dig out the images, feelings, and the nuggets of gold of your life. You might also discover a rock, a forgotten ring, a love letter, a music you once loved, a lovely film that broke you open, and a book you read as a child that still makes you weep. Think of your daily writing as a shovel. You are digging out the dirt so you can get to those buried, hidden treasures. You might also dig down far enough to reach China or you'll tap water that will carry you over to a new life. We use them to "jog" our memories and exercise our creative muscles. They will later be inspirations for the character work you do! But that's all for later. For now, just get into the "habit" of doing them.

"I remember . . ." Example:

> *I remember my great-grandmother, Granny, as she was called. She used to sit in her big chair in the living room and crochet while she watched "As the World Turns." She would talk back at the T.V. screen as the women and men did stupid things. She wore tiny, cheap flip-flop sandals and would hang one foot over the side of the chair and move her foot in a rhythm as she moved the crochet needle through the yarn. Granny was very magical. Going to her house was always delightful for me. She made the most ordinary chores fun. She lived in a house on Fincher Rd in Haltom City, Texas with her husband my Pappa. I remember being mesmerized by her photo collection that she kept in the bottom drawer of her vanity. I used to take the shoe box pictures to her and she would tell me stories about each person in the antique pictures. I loved hearing the story of how once when she was a flapper, she got kicked out of the dance hall for doing the splits. My Granny had courage and gentleness.*

We will learn how to modulate our "I remembers . . ." as we approach scripts, but for now, just do them once a day. And if you don't do them everyday, don't go crazy, just pick them up the next day. No one does this practice perfectly. We have a tendency to beat up on ourselves when we are in "process." We want so much to be the product.

Weekly Script Reading

During the twelve weeks of this course, you're going to be asked to read a script! It can be any type of script: screenplay, TV show (drama or sitcom), play, or, in a pinch, commercial copy. Reading a script a week allows us to continuously fill the form, a constant flow of characters, situations, and ideas come to us while we read scripts; reading a script once a week is keeping your hand in. When you are not "working" on a project, you are constantly working on characters. Acting requires us to do research on characters, on themes, and on situations. The reason we only read once a week is to absorb it, to make notes to ourselves. Don't be daunted if you hate or don't like a certain script! This is good! As you progress through the course, you are finding your own voice and with that you'll discover what you relate to and what you don't.

You don't have to stand in awe of any particular script. If you don't get Shakespeare or Williams, then don't read them just because "they" are considered the "*greats*." You might find you like more contemporary scripts (screenplays/sitcoms). But if you adore Chekhov or Neil Simon, follow that. It is vital that in this workshop that you start discovering what you like, what makes you cry or laugh or angry. So this is the second tool to awakening. If you have read scripts before, you might want to revisit some of your favorites or the ones you didn't "get" the first time. (Has anything changed for you?) I'm not going to tell you how to read a script because I want you to go on an exploration each week. Let this be an adventure for you.

The script reading is done for pure enjoyment. Please do not make this the old English class assignment. This practice is best done with the feeling of curiosity. We are peeking into our acting. We are just doing some looking into some books. Act like you are looking for things that give you joy. Don't spend a lot of time worrying about whether or not you're doing this right. There is no wrong. Just set aside time once a week to read a script. It sounds simple, but watch how quickly you get too busy or tired or whatever to do it. Part of an actor's job is to constantly read new material.

Don't read novels. No, don't read short stories. No, don't get a great collection of poems. Be bold. Step directly into your recovery. Get used to reading what you want to do. Surround yourself with scripts. I love to see actors have stacks of books in their hands when they come to class. It means their minds are always working.

Through your script reading, you are building a catalog, taking an inventory of what scripts interest you, what characters you would love to play (and they don't have to be parts you are to be cast in), and which ones you don't vibrate to. Write in your notebook each week: *which script you read, what you liked about it, and which character you would love to play. Why did those characters resonate for you?* Please be as specific as you can.

Charting Your Progress

Throughout this process, I encourage you to chart your progress. Continually, look at your strengths and weaknesses without judgment. We tend to say, "I'm blocked or stymied and thus I'm a bad!" I've learned to just say I'm right where I need to be and I'm all right. I can't make changes while I'm attacking my inner actor. When choosing between good or bad, always choose *good*. Look at the areas you want to improve and give yourself gold stars for all you have done.

Acting Practice

Acting practice is the process of doing. The moment you take an action, the universe responds. The minute you wallow, stop and complain, or dig your heels into the ground and stop, wait, and worry, the world responds accordingly. We can't trigger our good if we're lulling and procrastinating. We trigger it by actions (both large and small) done in a *positive* light.

> *Sometimes, you have to start small climbing the*
> *tiniest wall maybe you're going to fall but*
> *it's better than not starting at all.*
> —Stephen Sondheim

Acting practice is about doing—doing it badly, doing it great, and doing it just get to the other side—letting yourself just do it. This takes the high jump drama out of it. So often we put the cart before the horse. We put the "how" before the "what." We think we have to force our careers instead of trusting that if we stay on the road, the right and perfect parts will come to us. But staying on the road against adversity is what matters. Acting practice is about creating little dramas on the stage, letting us do it without the distraction and disservice or the worry about the distance of the end of the journey.

When you start acting again, you'll find it becomes automatic like breathing. You don't have to be good or bad at breathing, you just do it naturally. The same is true with acting practice. When you tap down, you are involved. You are not thinking. It's when we begin to intellectualize our acting with questions like "Where am I going? What am I doing?" that we get struck paralyzed and stuck in the mud.

I ideally want my relationship to acting to be one of love, one of joy. Acting practice can be done anytime, anywhere. We don't have to be "in the mood" to act. In the heat of living, acting will get done. Have a loving attitude to the part of you that wishes to act. It's so much easier for us to get to it if we have a lightness, a love affair with it.

You can do acting anytime and all the time. You don't need to give up your whole life or livelihood to act. This is sad news to most of us who believe we must let go of all worldly responsibility to act. "I can't work and act," so we worry endlessly about our bills. That's the price tag the we set and it often keeps us stuck in non-acting mode for weeks and years in some cases. Go steady and slow. If you're expecting too much too soon, you'll capsize. During this process (not product) go steady and slow (a house is not built in a day.)

Acting is not about ego, it's not about grandiosity, but it's about staying in the moment and taking the next right action.

Acting practice is about slowing down to notice what you have before you and working with that. It's getting there by small and deliberate steps. It's getting ourselves on track and making sure we stay on that track, noticing the obstacles and not being sidelined by the injuries.

Acting practice is the path out. What if you are in a dead-end life, have taken a major detour, and are far, far away from your acting dreams? Well, you start moving. Travel in stillness if you have to, but always keep moving. Practice everyday until you get it. Get what? Get it. Get good at it. Become "addicted" to acting. Become addicted to putting characters together. Grab a few friends and put on a show together. There is power in that. Let others (agents, producers, directors, and parents) show up when they will (and they will) instead of waiting for them. You will find that you'll be over and over again at the right place at the right time! The moment you wait by the phone steeping in anxiety, it won't ring, but the moment you get out of the house and do something cool, you invite that phone call or you meet somebody better or you realize how that phone call has zapped your energy (fuel). This is actually called "the law of attraction." There are many brilliant books, DVDs, and CDs written about the subject. I highly recommend *Ask and It Is Given* by Jerry and Esther Hicks and *The Secret*, DVD and book, by Rhonda Byrnes.

Acting can be done in daily installments (like paying for your house, car, or anything else); it's a matter of always being tuned in and turned on—what excites you, what do you watch (Pay attention to), what are you fascinated by, and what kind of story do you want to tell? Acting practice helps us to begin the journey into acting.

Don't be surprised when you start this process if you feel awkward, foolish, amateurish, and completely dorky. When we get back on the stage after weeks, months, and years, it feels rusty. It "feels" like we're not good. That is what we use to talk ourselves back down. We rehearse our first monologues and scenes, and we want perfection. I would recommend that you go for hours and even years of practice and don't judge your early work harshly. Think of it as planting seeds. You are putting them into the ground by daily writing and playing with scenes. Drop the expectations. We will do headshots that look terrible, we will go to auditions and fall flat, we will get dropped by agents who can't find a market for our talent, and we often point these early attempts as reasons why we won't succeed. Don't. Please. You are from now on to *encourage* your creativity and rack up the hours and miles and worry about how good or bad it is at a much later time. If ever at all! Soon, you will have the confidence and the proof that healing is taking place.

I want to encourage you to grow. I want you to discover your truest nature. What in you longs to be born (acted)? How can you bring those qualities to the stage? Or acting? Not just on the stage or the page of their work. What do you have that is so unique, so expansive, and so true that every time you use it, engage in it, you are tapping into your higher consciousness? At first, you might not know, but through practicing with these tools, you'll soon begin to discover it.

We all know the old adage, "Practice makes perfect." I believe the trouble is we don't get to practice—we always have to be perfect. Our scene work is not always looked at with tender, loving eyes and gratitude for all the hard work, no, it is appraised, criticized, and graded (how odd to put a grade on creativity!). How can you grade a working living piece of art? It's insane and ludicrous.

You can only gage it in terms of where the actor stands and where he is learning. We must always be in the process of learning even if we are seasoned actors. We must always go back to the beginning. Yes, you may have completed one game but you always go back to the start (this time with more playing strategies, more skills . . .), and it's perfectly natural.

With the practice of the two-minute scene or the one-minute monologue, we gradually get better. It would be very difficult for a singer or dancer to go on stage without hours of daily practice. Why should we expect acting to be any different, but we do? People always talk to me about my "gifts" and how "natural" my acting seems to come, but what they don't know is the many hours I spend honing my talents, the many years that I've spend watching, listening, rehearsing, and making mistakes. When I went back into acting, I had to learn how to treat myself kindly and go gently; otherwise, I would get discouraged and quit. So what seems natural and easy is only the processing of all that I have learned.

Acting Practice Rules

I grew up with so many rules. "Do this! Say this! Don't do that. You should look like this. Be on time. Do what everyone else says." So many rules that held me back, all to mold me and box me, and then I learned that the rules were always made to be broken—rules were flexible and written by people who wanted to manipulate me (either on purpose or by accident). Rules could be changed at the drop of a hat. And then, one day, I woke up and saw that no one was keeping score. No one was all that concerned. Nobody was grading me (except me), no one was going to give me a gold star on my paper of life, and this created a great thrill, a great sensation. It freed me up, released me. I could create my own rules, my own codes, and break all the existing rules (roles, I just thought). If I chose to, I could create my own standard. I was a leader, a warrior, and a survivor. I could also use what I have learned to help my fellow actors out! Now, I'm going to give you *my* rules to acting practice. These rules are not anything but guides for you to follow. Use them as a map, if you will. Mostly, have fun with them!

Acting Practice Rules:

1. *Never give up!*
2. *Keep it simple and specific.*
3. *Show up and be prepared.*
4. *Don't say "I can't."*
5. *Follow you heart's impulses and desires.*
6. *Keep moving, don't stop.*
7. *Trust your mistakes.*
8. *Have fun.*
9. *You're free to be the worst actor in the world.*
10. *Do one thing each day for your actor.*

Not only have I lived by these rules, but I've also broken them all. Don't be discouraged. I give you plenty of room to do them wrong. There is no right or wrong. This is good. It gives you an incredible freedom.

These rules became guides that I came to live by. I would read them before auditions, I'd read them before rehearsals, and sometimes during intermission. I had to give myself a wide field in which to grow as an actor.

The rule "keep it simple" is about not complicating your acting. Keep your actions clear in your mind. It is also to remind us to be childlike. Play. Acting is play. The more you play with these tools, the easier it will become. What people seldom see is that acting is a ball. But we are so caught up on how tortured we have to be. We have bought into the notion (not fact) that acting always has to be beyond us, something that we can't get to. I say all children have the ability to act because they believe in stories, in fantasy, and in imagination, but as adults, we get so heady about our acting, in essence we take it so seriously that we fail to have a great time. Acting is fun. Period.

Introduction

Contract

This workbook will change you, will give you confidence and power to act again if you have quit, and it will recharge you if you're stuck in the mud. Whenever we do an acting gig, we get to sign a contract (hopefully for lots of money!), and so I'm asking you to sign a contract right now to yourself and the course! May this contract be the first of many you'll sign in your career.

Actor's Contract

I, _____, am committed to undertaking the recovery and discovery of my acting. I understand that I'm on an inward and outward journey. I, _____ commit to the duration of the twelve-week course: the weekly reading of the chapters, daily "I remembers," weekly script reading, and the completion of each week's tasks.

I, _____, also understand that this workshop will raise many emotions for me to deal with. I, _____, commit myself to excellent self-care, sleep, diet, exercise, and pampering for the duration of the course.

_____
signature

_____
date

You might want to photocopy this contract and post it in the inside cover of your actor's notebook!

Note: You can do this course solo flight, but I recommend you find a friend or two to work through the exercises. If you are doing it solo, ignore the two-person scenes and circle back on them when you get an "acting buddy."

Week 1
Act 1, Scene 1

"Never give up," I told the graduating class. "Never give up" sounds easy, but it isn't.

"Never give up!" Does that seem funny to tell you, who haven't gotten started? That's when you have to be warned! I can't give up. I have too big an investment. It's when you're starting is when not to get discouraged. The last time I was at the Academy, the president said, "We feel you're not suited to acting. Don't come back." Well, you see who's standing here.

"And on that awful day when someone says you're not suited, when they say you're too tall, you're not pretty, you're no good, think of me and don't give up!"

—Ruth Gordon

Acting Is Healing

I had the idea for this book when I unblocked as an actor in 1995 after I mounted my first show *Divanalysis* that I wrote, acted in, and directed. I wanted to title the book *Doctor Theater* because I discovered that I felt healthy, whole, and complete when I was acting. It became clear to me that when I was "on" stage, all illnesses seemed to vanish. I could be very sick and get on stage, and I would magically be transformed and healed by the power of acting. After the performance, I used to joke to friends, "*Doctor Theater* has taken over!" What had transpired? What was this healing power? Was it the nerves of performing? Was it some weird psychic mysterious power that we tap into when we perform? Was it simply God, spirits or simply feeling good? I became very interested in how acting can heal our lives. I set out to not only explore them for myself, but see if other actors experienced this "healing" as well, and they did! Since that time, there have been many performances, many paths, and new methods that have revealed themselves to me.

I've been witness to these magical properties at work when we are acting. There is "something" larger than us when we act. It changes the chemistry inside of us when we tap into those energies.

I wanted to dive right in and tell the world to act. "Go for it!" I wanted to tell everyone! I still do. I unblocked using these tools and techniques, and I'm sharing those in this acting workbook. Blocks are caused by fears, angers, and doubts, and they can be dismantled. We can be healthy, productive, and functioning actors again if we tap into these healing, acting energies.

Through acting, each day, we get better. Acting is actually healing and healthy. I think we create dis-ease when we stop doing what we love and try to please others. I can't separate acting from living. What if acting could be done daily? Acting done daily while we wash dishes, fold the laundry, drive, etc. Set aside a small amount of time (about ten minutes) and use it to act. What I'm driving at is: don't wait for someone to give you money or a part. Act each and every day! It's a hard discipline, but the payoff is immense.

To me the whole process of acting is about changing the world around you. It is a magical power: healing, profound, and touching. You start off with the plan (the script, the screenplay, or just a bright idea) and you put together each piece of the puzzle until you have a complete form.

Rehearse a monologue for five minutes a day. We grow attached and distracted by the drama of acting that when we do it, we come to it with our defenses rallied. "We would take chances if . . ." we say.

The method of acting will be your method, whatever works best for you. I call my workshop "take what you want and leave the rest" method. I believe what works for one actor fails another, and we aren't given credit for our individual paths. You cannot train acting by teaching conformity. There is this idea that we have to force our acting and "concentrate." It stops the flow. The secret truth is that what works for you is best. If you find a certain tool useful, use it.

Each time we act, we get better. It becomes easier and effortless. I'm not saying that acting is easy and not difficult work. It does take you deep and that's one of the reasons we avoid it so much. We don't like the dark and turbulent and joyous and festive longings of our creativity. But when we treat it all like a process (precious), it takes the weight off you. Acting is actually natural and fun, but our egos demand that it be difficult and scary. Acting can be enjoyable and that's what I want to explore in this workshop. Acting is playing dress-up, make-believe, house, or postman. We forget this very simple fact.

It's difficult for us to divorce ourselves from our acting, but how many of us have tried? We stay in denial about what we really want to do while we stay enslaved to what we must do. Give up the thought that acting must be duty and think of it as something you love again.

Acting is healing; *not* acting is deadly. And by acting I don't mean you need to be in a film, sitcom, or play. I've learned the hard way that I need to act all the time so I don't get rusty. You want to use acting practice so you stay in shape, so when you get cast, you're conditioned to play it. It's very much like going to the gym. Let's say you are twenty-five pounds overweight and you start to workout. Well, you're not going to get in tip-top shape and run a marathon in ten days! You have to build up to it. I remember when I first started working out my first day on the StairMaster was *hell!* I thought I was going to faint, but I started slowly and one session at a time; I rebuilt my body!

I've learned that the more I act, the better I feel. I feel so healthy when I'm acting. Acting makes me feel good. I feel ten feet tall when I act. I know I'm large when I act because it is a spiritual experience for me. I seem to lose myself and become someone else when I act. I become excited. I find that I'm most depressed when I don't act. Depression is just a form of submergence, a drowning of our true desires. Depression is the deep, darkened water of our soul. We know what we want, we know who we are, what we are supposed to become, yet we spend so many hours, minutes, years, and decades discounting and distracting ourselves. In essence we are looking the wrong way.

Let's Start at the Very Beginning . . .

Where do we begin to recover ourselves as actors? We start with the self. We start within and then go without. We begin with recognizing that acting has been our dream, our desire, but we have gotten off the path. We begin to examine for ourselves the notion that we have invested in other people's lives and not our own careers. Acting is a revolutionary art form. We must revolt against the doubters and break existing limits.

We must recognize we are the mold. Acting is a gift we were all born with. It was god-given.

> *If you want to work on your acting, work on your life.*
> —Anton Chekhov

We seldom recognize our unique power. Instead, we ask everyone else and look for ourselves outside of ourselves. This is very painful since nobody knows who we *really* are and what gifts we were endowed with at birth. We spend so much of our lives trying to fit into a mold that never did belong to us. We wait for instructors, friends, and agents to point out our gold while our true potential lies dormant, asleep inside of us.

Who gave (gives) you permission to act? Nobody? Well, I give you permission. No, allow yourself to become what you wish to become. You'll ultimately become freer and happier and richer when you do what you love. Remember this: It is *your* life!

A career in acting is a process, not a product. And how many times do we confuse the two. "Oh, I'll act when . . ." and fill in the blank with any old excuse because they are all worthless and used to avoid getting to the stage. Think of your career as a bicoastal drive with many detours, many fun-filled adventures, and a journey, but the result is the end. Don't get caught up in the car that you are driving and comparing (despairing) about what others have or don't. We must keep driving. Keep moving. It's easy to see the mile markers and to stay in a safe town for a couple of years instead of moving on. We are the ones who choose to stop along the way and concentrate on the roadside attractions. Take a peak, stop long enough to eat, to go for a swim, but never-never stop moving. Drive or walk on. That's the only way to it. And be dogmatic about it. Don't settle. If your heart tells you to go for the big dream and you have the talent (or suspect you do), don't settle in to that teaching job that is safe but sorry. Stay on the road.

If you are teaching acting, directing, or stand-up comedy, then you better be living it. Share with your students the struggles *you* have. That will help them more than a head of theories, notions, and criticisms. I try to share with my students the good, the bad, and the ugly of my experience. I've learned most from acting teachers who are in the trenches acting.

WEEK 1, ACT 1, SCENE 1

Don't Show Off, Show *Up!*

Here's the "secret" of what I teach. Show up! That's the magic wand! That's the key to the kingdom. I've been studying actors for years and that's the one thing that keeps them from acting. They don't show up. They show off their headshots or talk to their friends, but they, when the going gets rough, fall out. Trust me there are about ten thousand excuses on any given day to not show up. I never said this was an easy thing to swallow, but the sooner you make it a habit to show up and do your work (or play), the sooner you're going to see results.

You don't feel like it. You don't feel good. You have all these fears that plague you day and night but you show up! You stand your ground when you show up. You lose the battle when you run for cover. You show your cowardice when you shrink back down. I'll bet you ten to one Jesus didn't feel like showing up a time or two. I'll wager Gandhi didn't want to show up or Thomas Edison, Buddha, Lincoln, Thomas Jefferson, Groucho Marx, Uta Hagen, Bette Davis, Michael Jordan, Meryl Streep, Bette Midler, etc. The list goes on and on. I'll bet they were scared out of their minds, but what made them great? It was their ability to show up when they didn't feel like it or when the odds felt overwhelming. Edison tried ten thousand times before he invented the electric light bulb.

I know on the days when I felt tired, bitchy, angry, uninspired, and good old-fashioned sick and tired, I've cashed in brilliant performances. This is a theory and not something I can prove, but when we perform anyway, the greatness kicks in because we have more at stake. There's more at *risk*. So the more you find yourself not wanting to show up, the more you need to force yourself to your scene work or your audition (or even the tasks in this book).

As actors, we often want to show off how good we can do something. This is asking us to preen like peacocks in front of a mirror. We parade our learning, method, or technique on the stage and it obscures the character. We don't want people coming up after the performance and applauding our techniques or method. We want people to say, "How in the world did you do that!" Acting is a magical process.

Let's say you've had a fight with your girlfriend and she's your leading lady. You hate the whole cast, your costume is three sizes too big, your shoes pinch, and you have a migraine, etc. Get with it! Show up! Am I being harsh, too narrow-minded? Yes! Actors need more toughness when it comes to this little ditty: Show up! Show up with a smile on your face, hum "Get Happy" if you've got to, but show up and you'll win. That's a number one reason why people fail. They don't show up!

So show up and you'll win!

That's It! I Quit!

Let's begin with discouragement. (I know, *ouch!*) We become frightened, angry, discouraged, and we quit. It's true. We do. This is a very difficult profession filled with "impossible" odds, fierce competition, and it takes incredible courage to keep at it. Sometimes, actors have it together and get famous at twenty-one, while others take years to come true. Often, it takes many, many discouraging moments to develop enough ego strength to demand all the attention to move center stage and claim that glory. There are many reasons to stop acting. I know, actors are supposed to have tough skins and be able to bounce off any and all discouragement, but that is not always the case. I wish I had that kind of power, ego-based energy, but most times, I have to be nudged along. I recently talked to a friend who was "crushed" because the show she was auditioning for was "pre-cast," and she did not get the part she had her heart set on. She was ruined and said she actually threw her headshots away and was going to get a "real" job! I understood her pain. I also gave her a dose of "never give up!" I said, "You take those headshots out of the trash and you go to any audition you can find." Well, she *took* my advice and the next week she was cast in a better part! The task I ask you to do now is write out some discouraging moments.

Complete the following sentences ten times:

I quit acting because_____.

What did your list look like?

Here is mine:

1. I quit acting because I didn't make any money at it.
2. I quit acting because my agent dropped me.
3. I quit acting because I got bad reviews.
4. I quit acting because I didn't like the acting teacher.
5. I quit acting because I was criticized by my friend.
6. I quit acting because I didn't get cast in the role that was mine.
7. I quit acting because my parents didn't support me.
8. I quit acting because I grew too old.
9. I quit acting because I needed to make a real living.
10. I quit acting because I didn't believe in my talent.

Does your list look a bit like mine? We all have something of the same list, I'm sure. Discouragement is hard. Often, we don't acknowledge our pain, and it becomes hard scar tissue that we ignore or forget about. We can't expect to discount our pain and bury it and forget about it, but those acting dreams don't die, do they? No. What happens is we stop believing and we shut off our creativity, and our lives become difficult, depressing things to live.

The trick is to repair our broken bones and start walking once more. This does *not* happen overnight. I'll repeat (for the impatient ones): This does *not* happen overnight! It's important to be gentle and kind with yourself. We think we must get tough and mean with ourselves and criticize ourselves and just *"get with it,"* but this only creates more anger, fear, guilt, and frustration. So I urge you to go steady and slow until you rebuild your courage backup. Take it from me, there will be setbacks. There will be times when you want to throw in the towel, but we now know enough to *not!* Right? Good. Acting was once our passion and it can be again over time. With small and delicate steps, we'll piece you back together again.

Often, we forget that we are actors at all! We forget the game and we stop playing. If we've been damaged, hurt, and shamed, we stall out on the side of the road. We let small things stop us:

Now let's make another list.

Finish the following ten times:

I still want to act because_____

1. I still want to act because I want to make money.
2. I still want to act because I want to be on Broadway.
3. I still want to act because I want to be on a sitcom.
4. I still want to act because I'm damned good at it.
5. I still want to act because my parents don't want me to.
6. I still want to act because I know I can make it.
7. I still want to act because I'm cute.
8. I still want to act because it beats the day job.
9. I still want to act because that acting teacher was wrong.
10. I still want to act because I deserve a home in Malibu.

Did your list kind of look like mine? Good. See, we're starting to find motivation again. This is fire, or at least smoke. Where there is smoke, there is fire. Now we just need to throw some firewood on. We need to get the sparks flying again.

Canvas State

We are going to try our first "acting" task. Take a deep breath. I want you to discover the basic part of yourself. I call this the "canvas state," the place where you are expressionless, blank, and ready to be painted upon. The first scene that I ask actors to do is *not* from a script written by someone else, but by them! I ask them to do it to find out they do have untapped energy. I've watched students cry, laugh, get mad, and even become children again while doing this exercise. No matter what comes up for you, it's *yours!* Honor it!

Do a one-minute "monologue" beginning with the sentence "I remember . . ." Speak it out loud. When you get stuck, go back to speaking "I remember . . ." You might tell one story or ten little one-line stories, just do it for one full minute. Don't worry about keeping to the facts or telling a "real" story or making it funny. Let it flow from your body.

When you finish, write down your results in your acting notebook and record how you felt. Where was your fear? (In your stomach? Did your hands get clammy?) Did you feel distracted? Distant? Vulnerable? Did you feel funny? Like laughing? Did you have fun? Or did you feel hatred, anger, or blame? Or did you feel stupid and freakish? What story did you find yourself telling? It's probably very important material and part of your "Vein of Gold." We will explore this topic further in the chapter.

I remember teaching this tool to a very secure, centered man, and he told a story of the time he stood up to his drunk mother who was preventing him from going on an exchange program to Europe. Anger, frustration, and shame all rose to the surface, and he clenched his fists and shouted at her through gritted teeth. The entire room felt the emotion within him. That is the rage of King Henry in *The Lion in Winter* when he denounced his sons.

After completing the exercise, write in your notebook for one page, "I felt . . . ." If you are doing these tasks in a group, have other actors write out the POSITIVE things they felt about your first acting. Have them give you these little notes of praise. Consider these your first good reviews. See how easy acting is?

Scene Observation

The reason I ask you to write about your scene first is to strike at it while your mind is fresh. The senses haven't been shut down by that old critic and the mental clutter of the intellect that numbs our work. Sometimes, the work might be good, but we are in a bad mood and can't see the value in what we've created. Or we may be in a great mood and an expanded mind and can't see the limitations of what we've done. Remember, above all, you're creating a huge body of work with your acting and writing. Don't be fooled by that censor (I call mine a dinosaur) that tells you what you've done is of no value. Or the one that tells you that you are great (that will only make you lazy). Some days, you'll do inspired work where you feel all the artist's muses surrounding you and others you'll feel like you're trudging through mud. Don't pay attention to either side. You won't win. Just keep practicing. If you do favor one side, listen to the part of you that says "brilliant, wonderful, and great." Am I encouraging you to be ego-based and self-centered? No, but I'd think positive thoughts about yourself rather than negative.

The worst actor can learn something from the best and the best can learn from the worst. The moment we begin to worry about the outcome of the product, we are sunk in the swamp of the results. The ego wants instant results instead of a building process. The mind wants perfection while the soul wants a journey. What a division! The ego demands perfection and is impatient at learning. The mind wants us to already know. We must relearn, retrain ourselves to go slowly. This is not good news for those of us always pushing and trying to achieve accomplishments. We scare ourselves out of acting before we ever begin. We set the jumps or stakes too high which makes us afraid. When we trip ourselves on these jumps, we become more fearful.

When we watch each other, it's important that we focus on the positive. How do we give positive feedback? We tell each other what we saw. We write down what we saw. Not in a critical, judgmental way, but in specific recall. Tell the actor what you saw them do. This can be difficult when we start, but once we get into the habit, we can master it. Don't write what you "think" about the acting or what you "feel" about what you witnessed. Leave your critical opinion in your mind. Don't tell them what to change, just say what you saw. "I saw you attack her on that line." "The conflict was clear to me." We observe the acting that takes place on the stage without judgment. This can be threatening to our rational, critical mind. We are practiced at telling each other what is missing or wrong with the work, not on what can be built upon. Does this mean we never say what is "bad"? Yes. There is no "bad" in acting practice. You get better each time you act. The trick to making your acting better is by being willing to be a bad actor. Now, when you focus on the good, the actor can begin to focus on those specific things. Actors are very susceptive to negative comments. I was teaching this exercise to a class and one student made an irresponsible remark about another actress, and the actress started to bawl and never came back to the workshop. I think it's time for the harsh method of "you don't get anything right" to die. Actors are strong, not weak. With practice and patience you get better. It's important that we remember to be patient with ourselves and each other when we act.

WEEK 1, ACT 1, SCENE 1

"Off-Hollywood"

I was the founding member, artistic director, and a writer-actor of a theater company that I walked out of in a fit of rage. I put my heart and soul into the theater company called "Off-Hollywood" only to have the entire thing blow up in my face like an A-bomb. After nearly a year of devotion and hard work, I was *still* being sabotaged by other members in the company who were lazy (and my friends) and not willing to listen to me. I was playing Bette Davis in a production called "The Tippi Trap" that my friend had written, and I was standing on a black block, lip-synching to a recording made off the TV, and I finally felt the salt of humiliation hit me, and I said, "I can't do this! I quit." I'll admit that it was not the most professional thing in the world to do, but I was forced by knifepoint into an impossible corner. I couldn't get the playwright (and friend) to see reason that his show needed some major reworking and cutting before we put it up publicly, but the other founding members kept saying, "Stephen, you are oversensitive! Just be quiet! It's okay."

I thought I had a good leg to stand on as the last show that I did for them was *Legends and Bridge* (the first act of a play about Joan Crawford, Bette Davis, and Judy Garland), which was sold out and got great reviews. The problem was the people at the top did not want me to "work for them." Instead, they wanted to keep a friendly little club together, not a *functioning,* highly organized company of "professional" actors. Everything was run by *ego* and feelings (including me) instead of insisting on quality work and the cultivating of talent. I had to cut ties with many associations in that artistic environment as they were so toxic to my actor. It was intended to be a place where my friends and I were to cultivate each other's work and in addition give me a place in which to craft my acting course. But things did not go according to my ideals. I found more harm, danger, and backstabbing than I did creativity and encouragement. I'll share the review here not to place blame, but to show that sometimes when you deal with others you might be *right.*

Backstage West review by Wetzel Jones

One wants to be glib and compare this to a train wreck, so filled is it with moments at which you can only stare in fascinated horror. This gives, however, short shrift to the train wreck, which at least has an inherently dramatic structure. Christopher Reidy has a nugget of a good campy idea here, that of having Alfred Hitchcock direct the Walt Disney Picture, The Parent Trap. Joining the master of sublimated desires to a film that was nothing but flagrantly advertised motivations seems inspired. This all gets lost in the soapy exposé of "Tippi" Hedren, who is going to tell us "Hollywood story." She then goes on to relate her tale of abuse at the hands of Hitchcock during the filming of The Birds and Marnie. Meanwhile, Hitchcock has rewritten the Disney project, called it Prying Eyes, and stocked it with Joan Crawford, Bette Davis, and, when Hayley Mills gets yanked from the picture by Walt Disney due to the inappropriate vehicle it has become, Tina Crawford and Patty McCormack as the twins.

Walt Disney, it should be mentioned, is represented as being in a rather unwholesome relationship with Marilyn Monroe. Truly embarrassing lip-sync numbers are staged for no apparent reason other than to bloat an already disjointed and plodding production. Watching Joan Crawford, Mills, and Monroe stumble through "Sisters" is to witness one of those dreadful moments onstage at which time you feel a moral imperative to stand up and demand, "Stop! Stop! For the love of God, stop!"

While there are no bright spots, it should at least be noted that the Monroe character shows consistency, if not a lot of texture (was even Marilyn Monroe Marilyn Monroe all the time?). Though the script is not loaded with quotable exchanges, it includes one that haunted me as I slunk out the door: "Can I open my eyes now?" "Yes? it's over."

But eight years later, the film that starred me was called *Off Hollywood*. In it, I played a goofy character named Davis Davis who was obsessed with saving Hollywood. God has a wicked sense of humor just like mine. I had gotten the part of Joanne in *Come Back to the Five and Dime, Jimmy Dean, Jimmy Dean* and had no time for another audition when I got the notice from my agent to be seen *again* for a movie called *Off Hollywood,* and I sort of breezed in, read my lines, and ran out. On my birthday, October 2, I got the following e-mail:

Dear Stephen,

It was a pleasure meeting you last week at your audition for the role of Davis Davis in OFF HOLLYWOOD at Sandwick Films. We appreciate your attendance. This movie, which I co-wrote and will direct, is a true "passion project" with everything on the line. Our expectations for it are very high and our company has gone to great lengths at every point in its development to ensure that the project's independent spirit and integrity are not compromised in any way.

As you remarked in the studio, we have been casting the male lead for a long time, (since May). Dissatisfied with our options at summer's end, we chose to postpone the shoot and continue casting instead, without our casting directors. Time and again they had recommended actors who I felt lacked the personality and presence that the role of Davis requires to live and breathe, as it should.

They apparently figured you could not carry our film. I do not share that opinion.

We secured financing for this 35mm feature film outside of the industry so that we could exercise complete creative control over every aspect of the production, including, as it concerns you, the cast.

With due respect, though I do not believe that your performance as Davis to this point has been anywhere near your potential, I saw enough the other day to be encouraged and entertained by some of your more confident moments. I hope you agree that with the proper commitment from the right actor that there is a world of potential in the character of Davis in this movie.

Davis is the missing piece of our puzzle. With the right actor in the lead I believe that OFF HOLLYWOOD will be a genuine success, creatively and commercially. Though you might be right for the part, my producers and I need to be certain that whoever we cast is able to carry this movie without any doubt. The right actor must prove himself to us. Performing on-book, an actor will drift in and out of character as he refers to the script. To address that concern from your recent audition (and your pre-read), I would like to see you perform the sides (p. 1-10) off-book, with a firm command of the dialogue. This role is dialogue intensive and it must be performed as written, with conviction and passion.

I have surmised that you are looking to move your acting career into the mainstream and that the time to do that is now. I believe that if you are willing to commit yourself to this material as an actor and trust the creative vision in place, the cast and crew around you will do the rest. Though this is a low budget "indie," the quality of the people involved is high and the vision is clear. (And it should be fun!)

The prospects for this movie are good, and the lead part is there for the taking. But the reality of your participation rests largely in your hands. If you demonstrate a strong command of the dialogue (verbatim) and deliver a steady performance with conviction and passion, your chances going forward will be good. You must know the material by heart, inside-out, backward and forward.

If you are seriously interested in this opportunity, let me suggest a thorough read of the screenplay to optimize the context for your choices in preparation for another performance of the sides. Our producers have informed your agent (who passed along your e-mail address) that we will plan for the week of October 15.

I hope that I have not been too forward or presumptuous in any way. If my direct approach isn't your cup of tea, let me offer my apologies instead and wish you the best in your future endeavors. Otherwise, I look forward to seeing you again.

Feel free to contact me with any questions at all.

Thanks and be well.

Joseph O'Donnell
Writer-Director

And this was my response to him:

WEEK 1, ACT 1, SCENE 1

joseph,

> *I don't think I've ever read such an impassioned "call back" email in my life. If you feel that strongly about me and my talent . . . I'd be more than happy to come in on Monday the 15th "off-book." I did feel like you did, that I was getting bits and pieces of Davis.*
>
> *As an actor, I am always looking for great roles and great films and I certainly do understand the importance of this film and will do everything I can to bring that vision to light. It's a very funny script and I'm a very funny guy so I'm hoping we'll mix well.*
>
> *I definitely connect with Davis' passion, drive and unbridled gumption to make his project work and to restore Hollywood to glory as I've shared those same visions! I even had theatre company called "Off-Hollywood." And for all my success, I did experience some of the heartbreak this character endures!* t*hank you for believing that I can do it . . . It's a great birthday present!*
>
> C. Stephen Foster

And then I spent the next two months auditioning for the role and finally booked it on December 20! It required more focus, passion, and determination than anything I ever invested time in. The director later told me that as soon as he saw me, he knew I *was* that character. I guess I am. I know what it's like to be obsessed, and I certainly paid my dues in *Off-Hollywood* camp. I can't describe to you the profound excitement I got the day I opened the envelope with the paycheck with payment for *Off Hollywood!*

I also spent the next three years making the movie. The movie went over budget after three weeks of initial production, and it took our director two years to get the rest of the financing for the movie and for us to wrap the movie. It was wildly exciting, overwhelming, and maddening, but I have a feature movie that I am the lead in.

When did I begin to book roles? Well, I did drag for many, many years! I wrote a show called *Divanalysis* where I played Bette Midler,

Judy Garland, Karen Carpenter, and Liza Minnelli. I wrote a play called *Legends and Bridge* where I played screen legend "Bette Davis," but it was the insistence of my partner Chuck that I "give up the gown" and show the world the *Stephen* he knew around the house (funny little guy with great "double takes")! It took years of urging, but almost as soon as I did, I started to book. I followed in the heels of actor Leslie Jordan who won an Emmy and was on *Will & Grace,* very funny, very short, and gay! He was the role model for my talent. So I started by going to a lot of casting director workshops, and in them, I was always given "comedy" copy and usually had the audiences laughing. That was a very good sign! And later, at Chuck's urging, I tried my hand at stand-up comedy! Well, that's when it started to click into place! Two months after I took my stand-up class, I was cast in a paying gig as a comedian in a burlesque troupe. And then I booked two commercials. And later, I was given my first professional stand-up gig by my old boss from Tower Records. Everything comes around full circle.

But how did this come about? Why did it take me so long? I think it was because I was not clearly defined as to what types of roles that I was perfect for until I started to understand my specific creative genius.

> *We can't take any credit for our talents.*
> *It's how we use them that counts.*
> —Madeleine L'Engle

Panning for Gold

I always worked, but that work never really manifested until I mined my true "Vein of Gold." I was good and funny and did great character work when I "dressed up" as Bette Davis, Judy Garland, and other women, but it was playing *myself* that I started to really make it! The term "vein of gold" is a term that I stole gladly from Julia Cameron (who stole it from director Martin Ritt) who wrote a book about getting in touch with your creative heart. It's interesting to me how we can be "miscast" for years, because we don't know who we are!

Here is what Martin Ritt said to Julia Cameron about it, "All actors have a certain territory, a certain range they were born to play. I call that range their 'vein of gold.' If you cast an actor within that vein, he will *always* give you a brilliant performance. Of course, you can always cast an actor outside his vein of gold. If you do, the actor can use craft and technique to give you a very fine, a very creditable performance, but never a performance as brilliant as when he is working in his vein of gold."

The "Vein of Gold" is something that you *already* have! It is your own personal gold mine. It is the part of you that separates you from the other animals in the zoo. If you are a monkey, don't try to be a tiger. All you have to do is uncover it from the debris of your life. Consider this an elaborate game of "Clue" you are playing with yourself (and other actors if you are doing it in a group).

We actors have more creative talents than we think. I want to encourage you to discover your truest nature. The first step to bring those qualities to the stage, TV, or films is to find them. Once you discover what is so unique, so expansive, and so raw, you'll begin to relish it, work with it, and learn to mold with it.

This is one of my favorite tools for mining acting "gold." I love to administer this little quiz to people as soon as I meet them. I've always marveled at how this little quiz produces starting insights. When my partner Chuck and I first met, I made him do this on a napkin at dinner. He was a songwriter and asked if the same would work with songs, and it did! This exercise allows us to break ground about our talents, our passions, characters we are drawn to, and themes of our lives. After doing the following exercise, you'll find the water in your acting life will take on different shades.

Task: Name your "Vein of Gold."

List your five *favorite* movies.
List your *favorite* childhood book.

Here is an example list of my favorite movies:

Grease
Harold and Maude
Star Is Born

Color Purple
Beaches

Favorite Childhood book: *A Wrinkle in Time* by Madeleine L'Engle.

What does my movie list reveal? It's a good idea to write this out (or have those in your cluster tell you what themes they see on your list). Here is what my list shows about me: music, female troubles, a reversal of fortunes, survival, destiny/fate, opposites attract, and teaching through life. Each theme, relationship, and character I've played or used in my acting and writing many, many times!

Now tie it together. What is your favorite childhood book about? In *A Wrinkle in Time*, a brother and sister travel through space guided by these spiritual beings who lead them to their missing father on a distant planet. (My own father disappeared when I was five years old, and you could say, I've been looking my entire life for him.) The lead character Meg discovers that all her faults are actually gifts, and she saves her brother by love.

Now I want you to dig deeper! Don't say, "I like that movie or book" or "they are funny." Really get in and do some investigation because it will reveal your heart. I suggest you do this within a group of others who will "see" things for you!

Now I call this part of the exercise "Oscar clips." Tell me one favorite scene from *each* movie. Do they have anything to do with *your* life?

Grease: When Sandy changes from goody-goody into the hot vixen.

Harold and Maude: When Maude and Harold are in the Sunflower field.

Star Is Born: When Norman tells Esther to quit the band and go for something "bigger."

Color Purple: When Ceclie finally confronts Mister and leaves him.

Beaches: When CeeCee confronts Hilary at the end for taking her friendship away.

Do you see any similar relationships, characters, problems, or themes? With your list always look for favorite scenes, favorite lines, and favorite songs because this is what *you* feel the strongest about! (e.g., In *Grease* I adore when Sandy sings "Hopelessly Devoted to You" and care less about "Greased Lightening.")

Do the same for your favorite childhood book. My favorite scene is when Meg discovers that love is what she has that *"IT"* doesn't and saves her brother Charles Wallace and goes back to Earth with her newly found father.

Now, here is another list of my favorite movies:

Ordinary People
Men Don't Leave
Little Man Tate
This Boy's Life
Amadeus

Favorite Childhood book: *The Giving Tree* By Shel Silverstein

What different side of my personality do these films show—a boy who has to become a man, a troubled past, mother-son issues, a nonconformer, a child prodigy who has a difficult time and conquers them, the misuse of power, and genius struggling in the world.

I might be laboring the point, but when you start to look at these lists, you'll start to find what kind of roles and script that suit you, what type of themes you feel most comfortable in.

So if you combine the lists, you'll see a boy who came up against all the odds who has a very creative and colorful imagination. This same kid has troubles with women and believes in spiritual assistance. So these are the topics that mean the most to me and are the roles that I most passionately play!

Here is another list of favorite movies from my student, Andrew. See if you spot his "Vein of Gold" before you tackle your list.

Amadeus
Lion in Winter
Harold and Maude
Casablanca
Monty Python and the Holy Grail

Favorite Childhood book: *Lord of the Flies* by William Golding

We have covered a lot of ground this first week. Give yourself a pat on the back.

Tasks

1. *Start an actor's notebook.* Buy a special notebook to keep your notes and tasks in. (You may wish to collage the cover with pictures you like or dreams you want to accomplish.)

2. *"I remembers..."* Everyday write a page starting with the sentence "I remember..." and write whatever comes to mind.

3. *Find a script and read it.* Go to the library or the net if you don't have the money. Just for fun!

4. *Putting the light on it.* Create a special actor candle. Get a very flattering photo of yourself and tape it to the outside of a prayer candle (I use the tall glass ones) and add an affirmation "I am a wonderfully, talented actor!" or "I am now being cast!" "Acting is God's will for me." "I'm willing to act." Light it daily.

5. *Obtain a small houseplant.* Nurture and care for this plant during the twelve weeks of this course. Think of this as your renewal to your actor.

6. *"Impersonations."* Make list of famous people and put them into a hat and pull one out and see if you can impersonate them. (This is best to do with your acting "buddies.")

Week 1: Check-in

This is to be done in your notebook. Allow yourself some time to fully inventory your progress and pitfalls. I recommend you keep these answers private and to yourself. If you are doing the workbook in a workshop setting, share these in a group of 4 people without "comment" or "feedback" from others. Each actor getting five minutes to share so no one gets left out. If you have an idea for another actor, share it with them AFTER class via phone or email.

1. How many days did you do your "I remembers . . ."? We are after seven days. Why did you skip them? (If you "Didn't have time . . . ," can you find the time? Even five minutes?)
2. What script did you read? What did you like about it? Did you enjoy the process? (If you didn't do it, why not?) Remember, script readings are important to building a foundation.
3. Any issues come up for you? What were they?

Week 2
Act 1, Scene 2

Who Are You?

The basic building block of your acting is yourself. You are completely 100 percent unique, and this is good news. This gives you a great foundation from which to build. What you look like and how you behave is the clay you'll work with when creating characters. So who are you? What makes you tick? What are your physical attributes? Are you shy? Are you outspoken? Are you athletic or a bookworm? Are you tall or short? Are you male or female? Are you old for your age or young at heart? Are you Southern or from Argentina?

All of these questions are very generic, but they help to decipher the code to yourself. It's a good idea to know who you are before you begin to create characters. The town you were born in, the family you came from, your brothers, your teachers, your home, your church, and your social circle have all been important ingredients in the creation of your most fundamental tool of acting: *You!*

Part of recovering ourselves as actors involves the work of digging ourselves out of "automatic pilot" or "just one of the team." We must begin to look for areas that set us apart, and we must learn to embrace them if we are going to claim them and use them. That is one of the vital things about writing "I remembers . . ." as it helps you to see different particles of you that create a full person.

Everything that has happened to you in your life is fodder for your work as an actor. Everything can be useful if you will harness it and put it to work for you. A hardheaded personality can give you the drive to succeed. On the other hand, a very shy, wallflower personality can help you play dark, deep emotional scenes. What you will discover when you start this sleuthing work is you contain elements of all persons, but you express them in different ways.

On the surface, I am short, funny, and have a high-voice, but I'm also driven, smart, and ambitious. So the two people can live side by side within me.

Are you talkative or are you withdrawn? Do you have a high-paying job or are you a waitress? All these things that you discover about yourself and even things you think of as your defects of character or flaws can serve you when you become aware of them. It's this dawning process that appeals to me as an actor. I think I know who I am until I bump up against a situation and I think: "Wait a second, maybe I'm different altogether!" And we do grow and we do change as we evolve as actors.

I spent most of my life pining about not being like other actors, and later in life, I realized it was a great benefit. And it was this difference that sets me apart at auditions and gives me attention in an audition room where everyone can look alike.

This sorting process will help you also help you identify parts of you that have been bottled up or kept a secret. For example, you might be a class clown instead of the schoolyard bully. These hidden parts are like little nuggets of gold. They will also help you later when you begin to "market" your talent. It's much easy to "sell" yourself when you give others an example of who you are. (I am a hybrid of Woody Allen, Leslie Jordan, and David Sedaris.) It will serve you in what roles you are best suited to play. It's much easier for me to find work as a comedian than it is for me to do Ibsen. But before I started to find myself, I would attempt to posture and act with false identity. I would always "act" a part instead of the character acting through me. I would cover myself up with costumes or wigs or furniture, but as I've shifted out of that, I find I have more range of motion and depth as an actor.

Look at yourself in an objective sense. Think of the creation of *you* as a very rare and valuable gem.

"Self, Come In . . ."

Identifying our true selves can be a little tricky. We often have buried ourselves beneath the surface of our every day lives. We can start to look for our identities by looking back at who we have already been. I have been teacher, writer, artistic director, lover, best friend, husband, administrative assistant, and enemy (just to name a few). Each of these "selves" was important to my self-definition. Each age I've lived I've been a different person. These roles gave me body and shape. I have loved playing each of those characters, and they each have helped define me as an actor. The hardest one for me to believe I could be was "actor." It was probably so big and large that it was easier for me to be something else. I was told repeatedly as a child, "Don't be selfish!" which translated for me, "Don't have an ego. *You* can't be center stage. Don't have an identity that makes us so uncomfortable," which was really mind-boggling because in order to be an actor, you have to have a sense of self.

We are often told that to be spiritual is to ignore your ego and just be selfless which doesn't serve us, who need the ego strength to endure the rigors of an acting career. To not have an ego is great if you're on a solo pilgrimage through Canterbury, but it won't get you very far on the Hollywood game board.

I'm not suggesting you to become an egomaniacal self-absorbed jackass, but understand it does take strength to define who you are. It does take some gumption, some ambition to be an actor. There must be a balance. If you have no ego or sense of your own identity, you'll always fall in line with others whims and notions. I developed my ego strength through the practice of writing and acting. I had many sweet successes and many failures but each one has guided me to a stronger sense of self that I continue to define.

So we begin to dig for ourselves through these games. With each stroke of the pen and with each acting game we play, we are finding ourselves. Start this week to look at your life for the various roles that you have played. You might also start looking to others for elements about their personalities that you'd like to adopt. Use your "I remembers . . ." to mull over these parts of yourself.

"Terrible, Toos"

Often, we are told by our families and society we are too much of one thing or another (too loud, too fat, too short, etc.), and we use these character flaws to attack ourselves. I was constantly told that I was too selfish and too impatient. These are actually assets if you can imagine them as such. How can you use the negative qualities to enhance your personality? List five of your "terrible, toos."

Fill in the blanks:

I'm too_____.
I'm too_____.
I'm too_____.
I'm too_____.
I'm too_____.

Inner Cast

Acting is in essence revealing shades of ourselves. We are not just one person. We are several people trapped inside one body. It's the expression of those characters that produces a change in the body. Acting is just revealing different aspects of who we are. I like to think of myself as canvas that I act upon. When I approach a character, I start with myself as a blank canvas in which I paint the character on. Even when the person we present on stage or in front of the camera is similar to us, we are still playing a "larger version" of ourselves. It is impossible to just be "yourself" onstage because you are playing a elevated version of your personalities.

I've seen many actors stall because they think of themselves as boring and their acting is like cardboard. You have to show sides of yourself you don't like when you act. Acting is visceral. Acting is tangible. We are at all times a cadre of characters. Observe yourself for a day (a week if you want to really go deep). On the phone, notice when you act or slip into another role. Do you tell someone a lie to make yourself look better? Do you not say something because you are afraid of losing a friend? What if the phone rings and you think it's your new lover and it's your mother who needs to borrow money? Now notice yourself in different situations. The acting class where you're intimidated by the teacher and you stutter and drop the script. Who are you at work around your boss? Who are you around the coworkers? Who are you when the boss walks in during a good joke? Who are you in a crowd: the wallflower, the go-getter, the funny woman, the wet blanket? How about the date you go on with someone you are not attracted to? And lastly, who are you when you are by yourself. Make some notes (without being strict or judgmental with yourself) in your actor's notebook. Notice traces of characters in yourself that are larger or smaller than you. Do you hide who you really are?

Inside of each one of us is a group of people. It's like multiple personality disorder in the movie *Sybil* starring Sally Field. I call this your "inner cast." This cast of characters can range from the Mr. Nice Guy to Hitler. We often have one "character" running the show, and it's usually not the most unique personality. We have many, many selves within us. It's good to identify these different selves and give them names. Julia Cameron calls them "Secret Selves" (from *The Vein of Gold*), and it's fun to look at them.

One of my inner selves is called "Orphan Boy" who is extremely vulnerable, isolated, and distrustful of others. This came from when I was growing up, and we moved all the time and I always felt like an outsider. I have another self called "Super Stephen" who just gets everything he wants. He's my hydra-driven self that sets a lot of goals and has little regard for what others think of him. And, in between, there are other selves that I let have a voice in my life decisions.

You might be leading your life with "Mr. Nice Guy" who does a lot for others and gives constantly and never says "no." Well, deep inside of you, there may be a "Selfish Stan" who is not afraid to get what he wants and can take and take. This side can be very helpful and destructive as well. You might have a "Lazy Lisa" who likes to slow down, take her time. Or you might be leading with "Crazy Cathy" who always comes across as scattered, out of it and belligerent.

There is nothing wrong with any of these personalities, but when we are led by one and keep the others locked away, we get out of balance because we are not expressing ourselves at our fullest potential. Name five people in your "inner cast." Start with your "dominate" self and go to the exact opposite.

1) write how each "cast member" helps or serves you.
2) write how each "cast member" hinders or limits you.

Imagination

Imagination is the strongest tool we have in our tool belt. If you contain a vivid imagination, your creations will have substance, flesh, and blood. Have you ever imagined yourself in a situation and then "presto" you were there? For example, have you ever thought about dating someone and the very person showed up? Or wanted a certain job and then you saw it advertised? These are forms of creative visualization. We create first with our thoughts and then with our actions. The two go hand in hand. See very clearly *what* you want, take the right actions toward it, and you *will* have it. Too often we use our imaginations to think about situations that do not serve us well.

I suggest to students to turn off the horror stories of the news, TV, and computer. I once was working with a manager who was representing one of my scripts. I called her one morning for a little meeting, and she said tearfully, "Oh, Stephen, I'm so sad . . . I'm watching the 9/11 fifth year memorial . . ." And I said, "You might want to turn off the TV if it's making you so sad." What I wanted to say was, "Turn off the TV, pick up the phone, and pitch my script!"

We are working on using our visualizations in positive ways in this book. We will be using our "inner movies" to create more of what we want and less of what we don't want. Acting is making a lot of things up and putting them into practice. We are always making up things in our minds (a lot of them negative), and what we're going to learn to do is write these positive "inner movies" down and watch them manifest. We are going to get our dreams and goals of acting out of our heads and into the world. As blocked actors, we often have very negative fantasies about our careers. So as we begin to recover, we're going to get these positive "inner movies" down on paper and start making them real. Imagination is a fantasy of the thing you'd like to realize.

We must begin to imagine that if we do our acting practice (our "I remembers . . ." and script reading) we'll be guided. Doors will slowly begin to open for us. It's the walking through them that requires faith, support, and encouragement. We first of all must accept we want to act, and then we must act on those desires. It's also our job to respect that we do wish to act and do the daily steps to walk to it. Instead of sending out fifty headshots, postcards, or letters a week, maybe we can do one or two. Keep it simple. Let yourself have fun in this process.

This week, grab a stack of magazines and begin to pull out images that speak to you—houses you'd like to live in, TV shows you want to be on, agents you want to "rep" you, cars you want to drive, and awards you want to win. This is the beginning of "seeing is believing." Paste these inside your notebooks with the feeling of "this is for me!"

Willingness

> *Ever since there have been men, man has given himself over to too little joy. That alone, my brothers, is our original sin. I should believe only in a God who understood how to dance.*
> —Henri Matisse

If it were my will, I would never have acted. Somebody or something else wanted me to be an actor. It has often felt to me like I was pushed into acting. I was a very reclusive, shy child, but I had a huge imagination. I would watch the Carol Burnett show everyday at my great-grandmother's house and think, "I'd like to do that!" I remember being in love with my Olivia Newton-John records and listening endlessly to them. In ninth grade, my life changed. We were living in San Diego, and I on a whim took a stagecraft class. It was the backstage and the advanced acting class combined. I remember we did an improv, and I got laughs and I was bitten. I was funny! It seems like whenever I want to stop acting another door suddenly opens for me. Against my will, acting opportunities crop up. A call will come, a friend will want me to do a reading, or I'll see a casting notice. I've had to learn to trust these signs and signals to keep going.

I had to turn my acting over to a force that *would* help me. I had to learn to step out of the way and show up at the stage, the page, the audition, or interview. This has taken patience, practice, and open-mindedness. I've learned to be a good (or at least functioning) actor by being willing to be a bad actor. When we are willing to act badly, we move out of the way. We must do our rough drafts and warmups. We must learn to not judge this early work. I grew up in a household where acting was not something to be considered as a living. I had to find ways of believing I could succeed at it. I had to start to have fun. I had to bring to my acting a sense of festivity and play. I put on little plays, just like my sister and I did in the backyard. I believe that when we step on the stage, we are engaging higher forces to work for us.

Ask yourself what kind of God (festive, creative, abundant, jealous, competitive, or angry) do you let control your acting? We need various levels of support for our acting dreams.

We want to act, great right away. We want to impress people, become movie stars, make lots of money, etc., all valid reasons to act. I believe whatever gets you on the stage or the screen then do it. But let's examine for a moment what happens when we produce work only for them. We want approval, recognition, and attention in the eyes of others. When I first started acting, my whole agenda was for people to give me permission to act. This lasted until everyone had a say in how and what I was supposed to do *except* me. Let yourself act badly. Let yourself be the worst actor in the world. Trust the process of simply getting up on stage or in front of the camera.

Isolation

And you've got to have friends.
—Bette Midler

In order to act, we are told that we have to do it alone. The lonely actor is one who makes it all alone with just cavalier endurance and the strength of superman (or woman!) We live in fear because of the told competition (the odds!) We are told how difficult "it" is to pursue an acting career, and we get caught up in this as opposed to taking daily, small movements (risks) toward it. So we break our isolation. We form little communities of actors whose goals are just to keep each other on track and functioning. Start doing scenes in your living room (My friend Scott and I did a whole gala evening of a show we were working on.), get together and read plays, and don't stand each other up! Find people you trust and begin to act together. Read scripts with each other, do scenes, write your "I remembers . . . ," and do the tools in this book (that's why I wrote it.)

What makes or breaks an actor is artistic support. You need to have somebody in your corner fighting with you, a friendly spirit unafraid to plunge headlong into the darkness of your creative soul. If creativity is a journey, then travel with special, supportive allies. These can be difficult to find. As blocked actors, we usually hang out with those who mirror our dreams back to us as impossible (other "blocked" actors).

There is no competition, no reason, to beat each other out. There are plenty of parts in the universe for all of us. We believe falsely that we have to be against each other and only out for ourselves. It's much more fun when we have fellow travelers, but be careful to pick those who support you and not deplete you. One student was in a creative U-turn, moved back to his hometown to escape his dreams. I remember calling him and begging him to come back to Los Angeles and be a part of my play. He came back and started taking my workshop and understudied several roles and, through a series of lucky breaks, ended up acting as one of the leads. I remember watching his growth as an actor. Every night, this very creative man would bring in a new prop, a new costume piece, or idea.

In order to act, we are told we have to abandon everyone and everything and become singular. This is a very lonely road to follow, the lone wolf process. We live in fear because of the reported competition. We are led to believe that if you are going to act, you have to give up your complete life to it. And we get caught up in this as opposed to taking daily movements. Find creative buddies. Form clusters around your acting. Be supportive of each other and let casting directors and directors and publicity people worry about competition. I've learn the hard way that going it alone is a tempting fantasy. We get tempted into thinking we must do it all by ourselves.

What is lacking is the feeling of safety around acting. How are we ever expected to act when we are afraid of the dire consequences that will happen when we step into the pool. We are deathly afraid of what will happen. The other deadly thing we do is separate ourselves from each other. We don't act together in tribes. We don't tell one another where it hurts. We are missing the secret ingredient—supportive friends. We need to be around other actors in order to rise. Doing it alone was always my nemesis. I had to change that. I found friends that I could act with, act without judgment, people who I could be "bad" in front of. We are missing community around our acting. Thinking we have to brave the odds alone in isolation is very damaging to our paths. It's so much more fun when you have someone on your side.

We suffer so much in silence. We don't acknowledge the painful things or enumerate on our numerous victories. We have this false belief that we must do it all alone. We don't gather as actors and tell each other what really happens. We start thinking that it was only our egos wanting us to act. The rationale goes like this: "*Oh*, well, I didn't get that part . . . It happens to everyone . . . who am I kidding . . ." and the downward spiral begins. We put the anger and frustrations on our own backs. When what we really need is a cheering section. We need safe companions to vent a little bit to. Fellow actors who say, "keep going" instead of "you should quit."

It is important that you break your sense of isolation around your talents and seek out a supportive tribe. It doesn't need to be a huge group. You can find support in your family, neighbors, church, support groups, and classes. You can even form a support group using the tools from this book. I taught many, many "Artist's Way" circles when I was unblocking just to keep myself unblocked. We would each read the chapter by ourselves, meet in the group and do the "check-in," and then the tasks for the week—sharing our results (without criticism). I can't understate the importance of having a "friendly" alliance! I even conducted groups online as well.

I urge you to seek out support. When I mean support, I mean people who firmly are in your court—somebody to tell you things are going to be all right when you can only see the misery, someone who loves you no matter how bad you look or seem, and someone who tells you that you still are great when the critics tell you not to act. Remember you are acting for your health, not theirs.

Seek out friends who support your acting recovery. Begin in your notebook to jot names of those who leave you feeling empty, drained, "hung over," and unfocused; who makes you feel safe, elated, and ecstatic; and who believes in you and your dreams? Be as honest as you can. Some people will fall into both categories.

The first person who must firmly support you is yourself. The inner actor is a small, delicate yet very powerful child who requires support and guidance from your inner adult. You must guide that child with all of you. It does no good to bully and beat up on that child (that's the ego); the child will retaliate and scurry back into the shadows. Fill the child's world with wonder and love.

There is strength in numbers. We are in an anti-art world and an anti-acting world. But we must change that. The only way we can is by proving it can and must be done. We are in a collective denial about our need for help, for our desire for one another. I think we are missing community, camaraderie, companionship, and connection. We live in isolated, remote caves avoiding one another when our true hearts have a need for love.

I recently helped a friend "unblock." She was completely isolated living in a small town in Canada. She was working on her "comeback" cabaret show. She had stacks and stacks of pages and about hundred songs. She was completely frustrated and burned out. She took a bold step and invited my partner and me up to her cabin in Canada for a "vacation." She really was in dire need of our help to get her out of the tar pit of creation. Chuck and I spent a week working with her, night and day on her show. She broke down and broke through many times that week. There were tears and laughs as she witnessed her "dream show" come to life. She now has a show that is the culmination of a lifetime of acting, writing, and singing. All because she was brave enough to ask for help.

Accidents/Synchronicity/"Lights, Camera, Action"

Pain is what it took to teach me to pay attention.
—Julia Cameron

Before we get too far along our acting path, I want to draw your attention to the "bread crumbs" that will guide you along your path. Julia Cameron talks about it in *The Artist's Way* as synchronicity or "the fortuitous intermeshing of events in an unexplainable, but *noticeable* fashion." This seemingly accidental force really caught my attention when I started to put my first show *Divanalysis* together, and I had *no budget*. I was doing the tools in *The Artist's Way*, and I went into Circuit City to buy a new boom box, and the clerk who waited on me said that he had a theater, and I said, "I have a show!" I did *not* have a show! I only had these little skits that my friend Scott and I played with while working at Tower Records. Some other voice must have spoke through me because I found myself committed to doing my first play that I cowrote and acted in. My weekly income was roughly $146, and I needed to get a trunk full of props, costumes, flyers, and an antique microphone for our show.

I never had any belief in what Julia Cameron was talking about, but I saw it with my own four eyes! Within a month of when I first told the owner of the theatre that we had a show, I found *everything* I needed. Friends gave me costumes and props they were throwing away. I needed a 1970s Divine Ms. M wig that was red, curly, and moved like hers, and I had a friend who traded a thrift store some old clothes for the perfect wig we found in a box. I purchased my Judy Garland 1950s microphone (including stand) for $75 at a swap meet, and a friend gave me the perfect pale Judy dress and jacket. A friend of mine worked at a print shop, and he designed my program and used the company paper for printing them.

What amazed me is the objects came to me *exactly* as I had "envisioned them." I felt like I was witnessing miracles, and I was! I've seen these many things happen over and over too many times to discount them. I finally understood about being clear about *what* you want and allowing the universe give it to you!

I call this "coming into alignment with the universe." There is a great book called *The Game of Life and How to Play It* by Florence Scovel Shinn with a quote, "If you can wish without worrying, you'll demonstrate perfectly." In this book, she says we often *block* our good by trying to "figure it out" or by "worry, fear, and anger." It took me many times stumbling over my own two feet before I *knew* the universe had a way, better way, of "giving" to me than I did, so it worked best when I stated clearly (you must know *what* you want) and then let it deliver the "goodies." And then I learned a real "winner": the happier I was, the faster it all came to me!

Right before they do a take in a movie they yell, "Lights, camera, *action!*" and then you're acting! This is done every time so the film and the sound can align. So often in life we are "out of sync" with what we want! It's like our inner movie is somehow "off" or the sound is out of whack (by this I mean our "spoken" words). We are either taking opposite actions of what we want or we're "talking" in a negative way that defeat the very "purpose" we have in our careers. This is *how* the universal law works as well! When we set our hearts and minds upon a certain thing and stay clear and focused, the universe will give us clues and direction or a "definite lead." That means, when you have a desire to act and you accidentally come across the audition notice or a friend offers you a "tip," please follow it. You're being handed help! If you ignore it, discount it, or "fight" it by arguing and trying to reason, you'll end up back at zero again. We only do this because of fear. It says somewhere that we have to have the "faith of a mustard seed," and I sometimes only have a fraction of faith, but it's enough light to see one step ahead of me, and that's all I need and it's enough.

Every thing in my life happened "seemed" to by accident. I accidentally met people who have helped me "make it." It is these accidents that have kept me going, knowing that one day I would stumble across the right things if I could stay open. I find that so many times in my life I have wanted my good to flow from this or that source, when if I stay open to the accident something better would be revealed to me. For all the times I pushed and tried to make something happen, God moved me in a different direction. I happened to say the line that way. I accidentally turned down the wrong road only to find the appropriate direction. I accidentally said the right words that someone needed to hear, just happened to be in that restaurant when she walked in. I was going one way and he was walking the other and we "ran" into each other. I just happened to go to New York City the exact same time as him. There are no accidents that we don't set in motion. I just happened to call that agent. I just happened to ask for help. I just happened to hear that poem or line of a play in the air when I was rushing to the gym. I was lost when I found the doorway, and I was the only one who had the key. It just so happens that we discount all these blessed accidents. We don't return the phone call; we don't thank the universe. We don't think the universe acts lovingly toward us. We don't take time out for ourselves. (That's why we do our daily "I remembers . . ." and weekly "script readings.") These small feats will lead our acting toward the ultimate good.

This week, in your acting notebooks, I want you start writing down these "accidents" that benefit you. Begin to pay attention to how the universal forces are helping you.

A discovery is said to be an accident meeting
a prepared mind.
—Albert Szent-Gyorgyi

Tasks

1. *Who am I?* Write a page of who you are. What makes you different? What things do you like? What do you look (physical description) like? What do you dislike?

2. *List five people who support your dreams.* This week find an "acting buddy." Someone you could talk to for support. Call, write, or e-mail one supportive friend.

3. *List ten things you could buy or do for your actor.* New headshots, go on an audition, new stationary, write postcards to casting directors, demo reel, acting classes, dance classes, etc.

4. *List five people who are negative or destructive to your acting life.* Even people who in small ways distort or discount your dreams. (Their doubts are weeds to your acting.)

5. *Buy new shoes.* New soles give us new souls. Go for a walk in them.

6. *Movie madness: Select your favorite scene from your "vein of gold" list and get a copy of it (get ready to perform it!)*

7. *Describe ten accidents that have occurred in your life.* Meeting my lover, getting teeth fixed, the phone ringing, etc.

8. *Tell me about your "real" self.* The self you are around people. Who are you? Give me specific details about your personality. Describe yourself in different settings. Do this once a day for a week.

9. *Make paper dolls from you "inner cast."*

10. *List ten roles you've already played in life.* (i.e., mother, husband, lawyer, teacher, cheerleader, brother, etc.) You might wish to do an "I remember . . ." on one of them.

Week 2: Check-in

1. How many days did you do your "I remembers . . ."? Are they difficult for you?
2. What script did you read? Remember that reading a play gives us a ground and fills the form. What characters did you like? What didn't you like?

3. Have you found some great images to paste into your notebook?
4. Have you noticed any synchronicity yet? What was it? Did any acting opportunities come your way?
5. Any other issues come up for you?

Week 3
Act 1, Scene 3

Toxic Block Syndrome

Imagine for a second that I just drew a triangle with equal sides. At the three points on the triangle are these words: guilt, shame, and fear. I call this the "Bermuda Triangle." As you face this week, you might find yourself battling one or more of these deadly foes to your recovery. You have started down the path with your "I remembers . . ." and your script readings, but you don't know *where* you are going. You can't *prove* that you're doing any good. You don't have the three-picture deal or the lead on Broadway, after all. This is natural as we undergo changes. These can be triggered in various forms: friends, family, or coworkers who think what we are doing is silly, selfish, or nonproductive.

I once had a student who was doing great with the tasks in my workshop when she asked me if her husband could come to class and "watch." I made the mistake of saying "yes" and the next workshop he sat in, and I could tell from his body language that he was *not* buying what his "little wife" was doing. The following week, she called me and sheepishly said she was not returning to the workshop. Another student, who got a ride home from them, later told me that on the way home, the husband "shamed" her with these epithets: "You're making a fool of yourself. You don't have any talent." As much as I told her how far she had come in a few short weeks, she never returned to the workshop.

These well-meaning people are toxic to your actor right now. Later, you'll be able to spot these things as attack, but early on, if someone breathes guilt, shame, or fear at you, you'll block. These three toxic emotions can feel as ugly and mean as a seven-story dinosaur.

When these doubts get triggered in us, we are like a pinball being banged around those three corners I mentioned above: guilt ("Don't be selfish!" bang.), fear ("You're going to get fired from your job when the boss finds out!" bang.), and shame ("You're spending part of our savings on a demo reel?!" bang.) Since we don't say anything about these little attacks we begin sinking to the bottom of the ocean again wondering why our dream of acting feels foolish. I'm going to be blunt here: these are forms of manipulation used by others to control you. There is no softer way to say it. If you fall for it, you'll surely "block" again. For now, stay on the course. Pretend you are a very, very strong racehorse like "Seabiscuit"; you're warming up getting ready for the race. Keep using the tools to stretch. You're not ready to race yet. You are the jockey of that horse. In the movie *Seabiscuit,* the trainer spoke very lovingly to his racehorse. I used to joke to the director of *Off Hollywood,* "I feel like such a racehorse, you should just give me a cube of sugar after each take." I'm asking you to do the same. Stick to the "I remembers . . . ," script readings, and the pages of this book. Talk to only those who are in your corner at the moment. It can be a temptation when we begin unblocking to share it with the world, but be careful, too much, too soon can unravel your progress. Remember we are rebuilding step by step, not in one fatal swoop.

Suddenly, Become *Too* Busy

One excellent way to take our power back is to do an exercise that I call "Suddenly, become too busy." This means you re-stake the boundaries of the things, people, and places that are taxing you and taking up too much of your energies. In order to act, you need your energies, your instincts, and your talents. If you're too invested in dramaramas (a term Julia Cameron calls "crazymakers"), you don't "feel" like acting. All your dramatic, enthusiastic energy is wrapped up in the dramas in your life and not the dramas you're attempting to put across on stage or film. You know, the helpless, hopeless friend that damned over dramatic actor in your show or the phone that rings off the hook (and I don't mean your agent.). Here's how you rearrange things: Start telling these people, "Sorry, I'm too busy." And suddenly all those troubled souls will seem to fall away from you.

I was once dealing with a dramarama who would set up times to see me and then call the last minute with some problem or other: "I twisted my ankle," "My car is in the shop," etc. This happened about three times in a row, and I finally started to say, "Sorry, I'm too busy to get together with you," and she seemed to vanish. But temptation to engage is hard; we like to cling to old habits. You'll learn to leave the machine on—your agent will leave a message. What we're in fact doing is unplugging ourselves (withdrawing or redrawing) from others to gain our own ground, to find, center, and calm ourselves. You begin to say "no" to others and "yes" to yourself, and your dreams begin to come true, you become stronger.

Anger is a sign that you are really on the path to recovery. You might feel jolts of anger this week and be tempted to abandon the process. We do get angry when we are not given credit, given support, or when someone else mistreats our acting talents. We feel the anger, but we are often so "nice" that we bury it instead. Anger is like a boiling kettle . . . it can scald you or it can be used to steam power your dream. The trick is to use it effectively. When you are recovering your acting talents, you might find yourself angry at a lot of people who have held you back. You can write letters to them in your notebook, talk about it to your therapist or friend or mentor, but stay on the acting path.

De Fence

What are we talking about when we're "defensive"? I like to think of defense as "de fence" or "the fence." When we are moving from the "stuck" victim position to the more active, positive role, we do have flash bolts of anger. These are "psychic" thunderstorms of the soul; tornado watches are in order. Lo, to the one who steps on our toes, watch out for the people who stand in *our* way! I had a bold, heroic rebel yell that I once lived by, "*get off my dress!*" and I meant it, too!

It's like the end of *Gypsy* when Mamma Rose exclaims, "Gang way world, get off my runway!" See, what is actually happening is we're moving into a larger self, and when we do this, people and things look and feel threatening to us. We are actually claiming our "new" states of consciousness. It is actually healthy to have these "mood swings," but I believe you get further if you think of it as a swing set and try to not be so "off with their heads!" This is a full glass of water to drink especially if you've been in a "powerless" state.

I remember at one point in my life when I quit a job that suppressed me for four years. That's a long time to be held back. I actually secretly called the place "Dachau" (after the worst concentration camp in Nazi Germany), and I went through a period of about four years in which I'd walk into a job and if anyone even looked at me cross-eyed with malice, I'd give them a good tongue-lashing (or "tell them how the cow ate cabbage" as my Granny used to say) and just walk out the door in a thunderbolt of anger.

Was I moody, unbalanced, angry, and defensive? Yep, yes, you bet! But what I've come to see is I was readjusting my fence. I was exploring and expanding my borders. It's like I was a tiny state like Rhode Island, and inside I wanted to be big like Texas. So, in essence, I was removing one set of borders and staking my new territory. I later learned changing didn't have to be such an electrifying situation. Now I calmly look at situations (as much as an artist can be calm) and go to a café, order coffee, and write in my journal or I pick up the tools of my creative practice: I'll dance around the living room with music blasting until I can think and act sensibly and sanely.

I warn against putting up electric fences; it can fry your assets. But sometimes, you will have to draw a pretty clear line in the sand and duke it out with someone over what you will tolerate. This can be frightening to those of us so used to playing "nice." I remember the first time I told someone their behavior was unacceptable. I felt like I was going to faint dead on the floor. My hands were sweating, my stomach was in knots, and my head was spinning, but the situation called for honesty. If I lied, I would have continued to hide my feelings, but by being brave and telling the truth, it opened the doorway to a conversation and to an apology.

What Are My Odds?

We are not powerless as we so often think. We are only "powerless" when we take "no" for a final answer, when we are looking at the others in the race and measuring our path and steps to theirs. Your path was given to you for a reason. The only thing you have total 100 percent control over is your output. The "outbox" on your desk if you will. What you put into the universe, you get it back. Your mental attitude is everything. Watch your enthusiasm level. Are you creating happily, daily, forwardly? Or are you complaining, comparing, and despairing? We are not powerless or hopeless. We are actually very, very powerful if we will trust and use that power.

I have an old tape of Judy Garland playing Esther in a stage version of *A Star is Born,* and at the beginning of it, she walks into central casting and asks for work and the matronly woman disapprovingly says, "Your odds are one in a hundred thousand. Do you still want to be in the movies?" Esther replies, "But maybe I'm that one." I cry when I listen to that tape because that's how we should be training ourselves. We must know that the odds are in our favor if we "never give up." I think because we beat the ones who *do* give up. They fall out of the race. I don't believe in odds. I don't even like the question. It removes us from the work. Our work is a constant stream that we must flow along in. When I hear the odds, I think of all the way I've traveled from Fort Worth, Texas, and to being the lead in plays and movies. If you just keep doing the work (play), you'll advance. Remember the tortoise and the hare? Do a daily action toward your acting and watch divine power take over.

I know a gifted (and blocked) actor who went to a very uppity university and played the game and got whipped to death. He always felt "less than" and out of the loop and has been begging for the entrance into the alumni elite ever since. In essence, he was waiting for them to "make" him or grant him permission to act. I think back to my own college days and the pain I endured always placing my acting into faulty human hands. I wish I had somebody to tell me that the power was mine. Sort of like Dorothy at the end of the movie *The Wizard of Oz*—the power was always hers, but she could not claim it.

Learn from the Greats

Acting is doing as I've already said. But acting is also not doing. Listening. Not simply to the other actor, but to everything. Watching other great artists, knowing and observing what they do, and seeing and hearing if you can pick up on great tips—who helped them? What gave them inspiration? Find out and try using some of it. Madonna said, "I used to take my song demo with me everywhere, and I would give it to anyone who would listen." Listen to what the greats have to say about what they were great at. I always say I learned how to act by learning how to *play* Judy Garland, Bette Davis, and Liza Minnelli. I had to get under their skins and listen to their stories and then "convince" people I was those characters. I became a channel from which they flowed. So even when you're in acting school or class and you're worried about your own scene or career, think about what you can learn from people. Observing is a highly overlooked tool. Look at what they do. Don't compare, don't despair if you're not doing what they are. Change it. Can you incorporate them into you?

Where do you gather inspiration and strength? What makes you go on? Even on the worst day, do you stop? I recommend taking your career into your hands always. You must always maintain the power within you. An acting career can be built upon being told, "No!" Think of it as an opinion. Think of it as somebody's option to not buy your brand of talent and make your motto like director Tyrone Guthrie's "*ON!*" That means we have no time to sit and stall based on what one or two or maybe a thousand people say. We have to act no matter what, no matter what the results will be, no matter if we have money in the bank, no matter if others think we stink, or if they think we are the greatest. It is the work that matters in the end!

I read and used Uta Hagen's book *Respect for Acting,* and always thought I could *never* understand her teachings. It felt like she was speaking of techniques so elevated and lofty that I could never live up to them, like I was always doing them "wrong." And then I saw her perform in New York City in the two-character play *Collected Stories,* and the light bulb went off. I understood! I *was* doing all those things in my acting! Everything she did was specific, honest, and even raw. I became very excited about my acting and the craft of it because I knew I was able to act with that depth while being funny. Every object she touched had a specific vibration, every cross she did about the stage had energy behind it. About five years later, I saw her in another two-character play *Six Dance Lessons* and lightening struck twice. In her performance nothing was vague. Every word and every intention was clearly drawn.

What I learned from the experience is: while we can pick up an acting book and study the craft in classes, what really matters in the end is how we use them. Ms. Hagen spent many, many hours in rehearsal and in practice at the HB Studio before she ever put herself onstage in front of audiences. It takes many hours of rehearsal and research to get a part "right." The audience must never, ever see an actor's "homework."

They are there for the show! They have bought tickets and want to be entertained, and so do casting directors, directors, and producers. They want to see a performance. That's why you do "acting practice" in privacy.

Watching Ms. Hagen was an eye-opening experience for me, and I went back and reread her book and this time I understood that what she is teaching is "practice."

Listen to what the great successes tell you about acting, not some acting teacher who gave it up because it was too hard and they found a comfortable paying gig teaching students. "The method" might have worked great for Brando, but do nothing for you. Meisner might put one actor in the moment, but insult another's senses. Improv might help some improve, but deflate those who "freeze up." It's not the school that made these actors great; it was their *own* talent and what they did with it! Why limit yourself to one school of acting anyway? This workbook is the method of "take what works and leave the rest!"

Now we will find some "helpers" for you. List ten mentors in your life. (No, you don't have to officially know them!) Next to their name, list at least two qualities they have that you admire.

My mentors:

1. My granny (traits: patient, loving)
2. Chuck Pelletier (traits: great singer, talented)
3. Joe O'Donnell (traits: great director, stubborn)
4. Bette Midler (traits: funny, sassy)
5. Judy Garland (traits: genius, creative)
6. Ruth Gordon (traits: talented, bold)
7. Madonna (traits: ambitious, rich)
8. Julia Cameron (traits: teacher, writer)
9. Charlie Chaplin (traits: funny, producer)
10. Napoleon Hill (traits: determined, focused)

What about these people do you admire? What traits do they possess that you'd like to develop within yourself?

Actors I admire:

List five actors or performers you admire. Next to the name, write the qualities they possess that you'd like to bring out in yourself. Know that you already have them (even if you've disowned them!). You might make an affirmation of these qualities and put them near your prayer candle or in your notebook.

Example:

1. Bette Midler—funny, sassy
2. Woody Allen—comedic genius, great writer
3. James Dean—great actor, handsome
4. Jim Carey—funny, famous
5. Madonna—multimillionaire, world famous

I, Stephen, am a comedic genius actor-writer. I, Stephen, am world famous.

An "affirmation" is a statement that you repeat to yourself that over time will become true. We mostly speak very negatively about our acting skills, and we must begin to reverse that. When you first say a positive "affirmation," it will feel like a complete lie, but if you say it often enough with enthusiasm, it will manifest. The positive spoken word is *very powerful*. The vibration of sound goes out into the universe like a radio signal, and it begins to pick up the thought and begins to give you what you have spoken for. There are three master teachers who speak in-depth about affirmations: Louise Hay, Florence Shovel Shinn, and Shakti Gawaiin.

Tasks

1. *Perform your favorite scene from your "vein of gold" list.* Playing both characters, write down how this felt. (If you're in a "group," perform the scene with another partner and then switch roles. Each one, write down in their notebook what they felt and saw.)

2. *Give Oscar speech.* Give your Oscar, Tony, or Emmy acceptance speech. Who would you thank?

WEEK 3, ACT 1, SCENE 3

3. *How many hours this week did you spend practicing your acting?* Keep a log of exactly how much time (even small things like mailing out postcards) you devote to your career. (Notice for yourself how much time you fritter away.)

4. *List ten times when you've settled for less, slowed down, or stopped.*

5. *List five different odd ball paths to approach your acting career.*

    1. I could go to "industry" parties.
    2. I could put an ad in "Variety".
    3. I could write producer letters.
    4. E-mail agents to get the energy going.
    5. Upload my demo to YouTube or Facebook

6. *What do you bring to the part?* In essence, what is so uniquely yours that you bring to a role (e.g., my size, my voice, etc.)? I believe once we truly accept ourselves as we are (our bodies, our hair, and our mouths), we can begin to see them as assets instead of liabilities.

7. *Name the suspects who stopped you from acting?* Name them. Don't be nice. Be ruthless. I'm asking you to be picky and petty for a reason. Act like you are running a police report on them. Name the crime. What did these people say to you?

    (e.g., my stepfather, "You'll never make any money at it!" "You have to know somebody . . .")

    Write about these people. Write about what you remember. How it made you feel? Give them a criminal name (my stepfather: barbed tongue) like in a cartoon. Put the suspect or culprit behind bars.

8. *Find a biography or autobiography of someone* you *consider a great actor*. One of my favorites is *My Side* by Ruth Gordon.

9. *Time travel: Write an "I remember . . ." from all your ages.* You'll have a completely different experience at 8 than at 29 or 105.

Week 3: Check-in

1. How many days did you do your "I remembers . . ."? Are they difficult for you? Did you try writing one from the character you're playing point of view? Try it this week.
2. What script did you read? Are you remembering to keep this practice fun? Have you spotted some great scenes yet?
3. Are you remembering to put images in your notebook daily?
4. Have you noticed any synchronicity yet? What was it? (Did any acting opportunities come your way?)
5. Any other issues come up for you?

Week 4
Act 1, Scene 4

And the fog's lifting the sand's shifting I'm drifting on out.
—Bette Midler

The Hunger

In your acting, there has to be a hunger, a wanting, and a desire. Our acting becomes flat, lifeless, and placid when we don't have a hunger. Hunger is a desire, a fire, and a fierce wanting BURNING in your stomach. If you are not hungry and have a white hotness toward your career, you won't even start. The hunger has to come from the urge to create, the passion that burns deep within you. You do possess this passion somewhere, but it has fallen asleep. We are in the process of waking it up.

Passion is like joy. It is contagious and it is catching. If you don't have a drive for your acting, you can turn up the heat again. What excites you about your acting? Why do you wish to act even if it's for no other reason than to make a millions dollars? That's good enough for me. Is it for you? Be willing to follow your passion—let it always be cast in the sea of hope, energy, and creative universe. If you are passionless, rote, and bored, guess what you're going to bring into the audition space and the movies you're involved in? Bingo. The universe will mirror that energy to you—enthusiasm, passion, and action, action, *ACTION*. We must continuously be stepping, marching, walking, running, jumping, and leaping toward our dreams, wishes, goals and careers.

But this action must be pointed toward a specific target (objective). As actors, we like to spend a lot of time dreaming, hoping, and wishing, but at some point we need to organize ourselves, form a plan, and start acting on it. Napoleon Hill (author of *Think and Grow Rich*) calls it a *DEFINITE CHIEF AIM*. Now, after only four weeks with this course, you will most likely not have a *definiate chief aim* because you have been so discouraged, but I want to plant the seed in your mind because I've worked with a lot of "blocked" actors who have tons of "ideas," but when it comes to *acting* on those "ideas," they falter. Why?

It comes from being afraid to take ourselves seriously as performers. It comes from allowing too many distractions to take us over. We are afraid to admit our ambitions, and also when we have admitted them, we've gotten shot down. But when you do pick the fire of your dreams back up, you create a velocity, a divine intangible energy that cannot be stopped until you get tangled up in someone's "no can do" energy. I was recently working on a project with someone and getting him to set a specific time schedule, a working plan was like pulling teeth. He wanted to stay in "idea" mode, and the project went on the shelf due to lack of forward motion.

We don't allow ourselves to stumble, to fail, to act poorly or even act in small ways because our fire has burned out. We have to be great all the time. This is why we take so little actions toward our goals. We don't want to step out of bounds, and we don't want people to think we are "pushy."

We are taught that to want something so bad is wrong. In society, we are taught to believe that if we only let God, we will advance. This can create a dichotomy. We can forever bob along this sea of spiritual crux that we don't push for what we want. We forget we have to work for it. "Faith without work is dead." I'm not saying that God doesn't have a hand in our good, but I'm saying that God doesn't work until we do. We take the actions and God moves us along. We must tend to our careers. Our acting is like a garden that we are consciously growing. What if we don't give it water? The plants shrivel up and die. The same applies to our acting. Acting requires a lot of attention and care. We must continually supply the needs of our acting.

We have been working on pulling ourselves out of denial over the past four weeks, and we have started to make progress. I find a lot of actors have a mild form of attention deficit disorder because the work we do is so sensitive and creative. We like to focus on so many things, so many people, and so many "world events" that we bring little or no energy to our dreams. I'm drawing this to your attention now, so you can begin to look at it if it's an area you need to work on.

It was a *big block* for me until I got cast as the lead in *Off Hollywood*. That solved it all! I worked for six months before I even stepped foot before the camera. That role obsessed me, and I had to shut out *every* distraction in my life (friends, family, and causes). And even when I got on the set, I had to ignore the demands of everything (crew, cast, and visitors) to focus on playing the role. The *only* person I engaged was the director. He and I shared a similar mission, and I was *not* going to let him down.

> *Freedom comes when you learn to let go.*
> *Creation comes when you learn to say NO.*
> —Madonna

When we are blocked actors, we like to keep ourselves beat up and scarred by what I like to call the "9/11 syndrome." This is the part of our ego that constantly loves to be in the throws of drama, crisis, catastrophe, and misery. You know the drill: "Oh my god! I have to get my headshots!" instead of picking up the phone and calling a photographer or a friend who takes really good pictures. Or better: "Oh my god! I have an audition! I can't do *anything* for the whole week!" We create big production numbers over the small and simple steps required by every actor and wonder why we have no creative engines left for the real big moments. This high intensity drama requires a lot of nursing and is a difficult enemy to shake. It's another bad habit we get into around our friends to prove how important our big dream is to us.

Why do we do this? We are avoiding the work. When just showing up is all the universe asks of us, we like to compound it with drama, drama, and more drama! We show up frantic, hurried, rushed, blurred, and crazy at the big audition that's going to change our lives that we are operating on half throttle. Half of our energy and integrity is depleted. Then when we fail to get the part, we wonder "why?" Instead, we need to remain calm and centered until the audition or interview and then let it rip with the drama that's bottled up inside of us. Part of recovering as actors is surrendering the "9/11 syndrome." Keep the drama for the drama. Save the production numbers for those glorious musicals you want to star in.

Often, when we think of acting, we think in terms of it being an emergency, instead of it being about emergence and placing one sure foot in front of the other. We get roped into the "oh my god" syndrome; instead of working on the work today, we wait (procrastinate) and then groan, "Oh my god! I have this to do and that . . ." and we stay up all night, worrying and fretting.

So the drama or crises blocks us, stymies us, and shuts us down. Turns us off and turns us away. Be on the alert for these "red flags."

> *This is an inevitable truth: Whatever you write will reveal your personality and whatever you are will show through in you writing.*
> —Brenda Ueland

I recently watched a video of a play I performed in—a show that had so many difficult challenging situations off stage. I only see how tired and burned out I actually was. How uninspired I actually felt. I could see it in my energy and in my face. I looked listless and forced into performing. I could see that I was more blocked and unhappy than I ever was when I was "officially" blocked. What happened? Wasn't I supposed to be happy? I was living my dream. I think it had to do with self-care and nurturing. I was living my dream, but the dream was breaking my heart. Due to circumstances beyond my control, I was not able to confront the negative people involved in the production. The director was afraid of confrontation, afraid to assert his power, and when I told him certain cast members were out of control, he skirted the issue and hid out in the light booth like a worried puppy dog. But this failure taught me a valuable lesson in failure.

A rule of thumb about dealing with difficult folks, tell them the truth, your truth, instead of running from the unpleasant circumstance or person and be willing to "have it out" if necessary. It will serve you much more than bottling it up and hating yourself.

Stay hungry and stay foolish.
—Steve Jobs

Snakes "Hissing" in Your Garden

People will not always be in favor of your acting. It's important to name our allies correctly. Even the ones closest to you will not be for your acting desires. Don't worry so much about them. Stop seeking outside approval, and advice. Your only job is to act no matter what people will say or do. (One day, you'll be called a "genius"; the next day, you'll be called "washed up.") You just keep moving, moving on to the next film, the next play, and the next scene. Make "next!" be your call to arms. You blow the audition . . . "Next!"

Don't hand your career over to people, places, and things. Remember you are the *only* one who can really get yourself motivated and fired up. You are the one who must be selfish. We are told it's wrong to be selfish. We are continually told we have to do service, sacrifice, and play nice when all we want to do is act. It takes great courage to slay the snakes around us. We are told we have to pay our dues. Hogwash. I believe you pay your dues by showing up for the work not by pleasing a lot of people. "It's what you do that takes you far . . ." Madonna advises us. And sometimes, we must be ruthless when choosing between others and ourselves. Don't fill up your life with meaningless, gossipy conversations and toxic, traumatic dramas. Don't allow anything that doesn't help your career in some fashion. Think of what you have to sacrifice is the riffraff of people, places, and events. Most of it is like trash that must be thrown away. Sacrifice means you have to give up the invested time of other people and place it back in your center. You are the core and the key to your career.

Never let anyone carry your dream for you. They will inevitably disappoint you. Own your dream. Claim your right name. Never let somebody project onto you how your work should look. Their advice is sometimes jealousy disguised as "I'm only trying to help you" when they want to control us. They use words like "because I love you . . ." What they mean is "I'm scared to take a risk and you should be fearful as well." Don't buy into it. The price tag is too high, and you'll lose if you don't follow your own heart and soul. We can feel it when we are holding back on account of somebody else. We feel lost and confused. We feel deflated. We feel an energy loss. When you feel like jumping, jump. Even if you fail, you still have all that good strength from within.

Advice for our own good can damage us. I remember when my show *Attitudes and the Dance* was closed I had a difficult time during the run of the show, and one of my long-time friends called and told me all that the show wasn't. "It didn't have characters I cared for. Now, *Angels in America* that's a good play." In one sentence, the ax was dropped on the nape of my neck. I felt ashamed, embarrassed, humiliated, and broken like a bad writer, actor, director, and person. And why did I write in the first place? "What were you trying to accomplish with the piece?" I don't know the answers to these questions. But I had to write it to get it out of my system because I liked the idea.

I just write. I just act. Good or bad doesn't matter. I do it to go on to the next piece of work. But the words she used bruised and blocked me. I forgot all writers do baby work. All actors do better and stronger roles. But support, love, and nurturing is what I needed, not advice giving and criticism. I had enough of that during the problematic production.

Patience and Waiting

I'm not the most patient person in the world. Ask anyone who has ever worked with me. I blame it on being born three months premature. It was like my entire life is based on, "Let's get the show on the road!" I've had to learn patience over the past few years.

There is a difference between waiting and patience. Waiting creates anxiousness, excess weight, and creates baggage. We make ourselves heavy when we carry the weight of waiting. You know the drill—waiting to get the headshots, waiting to begin the rounds of trying to find an agent, waiting to join the acting class, and waiting to get out of bed. Waiting is a holding back, a withdrawing—expecting things to come to us while we sit and stew lounging in front of the TV. Waiting is putting our lives on pause. Waiting is wasting time. When we are waiting on some person, place, or thing to deliver, we are not in action. Waiting is inactive and renders us panic-stricken. Waiting causes frustration, anxiety, and blocks creative flow.

Patience, on the other hand, is a sure, silent moving. Patience is the quiet side of you that sits still while the active side of you is out doing the rounds, sending out headshots, writing letters, or auditioning. Patience is the side that encourages you to grow. Patience is powerful. Patience is our soul's truest place yet we place it low on our list of attributes because we are so caught up in the waiting trap for something to happen.

> *If you want something bad enough,*
> *the whole world conspires to help you get it.*
> —Madonna

Waiting is that frantic part of you demanding that we have it now. Like a child stomping the foot. "I won't budge until . . ." And what we usually choose to ignore is the many blessings we have. We fail to look behind at where we've come from. At all the "gifts" we have at this moment. All the things we could be doing for our acting dreams.

Patience allows us to grow slowly and to evolve. It takes the earth time to spin from darkness back to light again, but we won't give ourselves that luxury. We have to be paid, box office stars now with nothing to support the claim. We wait, but we don't do the footwork. Even the smallest footwork will gain results even if the result is a risk and the feeling that comes when you take the risk. Patience is having the ego to sit down and quit tapping us out of the dance. Patience is the side that knows that wherever you are acting is right now perfect.

I know I've gotten into trouble when I've waited for people. I have lost many splendid opportunities because I've been waiting for the ideal package to show up, and I've discounted the blessings that I've had.

Recently, in a workshop, I had a student curtly remark "I'm boycotting the 'I remembers!'" as she looked to me for creative support. I could see her resentments sparking off her face. I could tell she was frustrated, blocked, unhappy, and unwilling. She was unwilling to commit to her own creative maintenance, unwilling to do the recovery work. She was in the spiritual dilemma some of us find ourselves in:

wanting help with our creative lives but unwilling to work for it. "I remembers . . ." help guide me to what I need to be guided to and what I also need to be guided away from. Watch closely when you are trying to abandon your acting practice. Something wonderful is afloat if you don't throw yourself overboard. Don't stop. Keep moving. Try not to capsize yourself or let other people stand in your way. I'm asking you to stand up for your actor and take risks so you can grow.

We are aiming at concentrating on small, doable actions we undertake and giving ourselves rewards and treats along the way. We don't need to beat ourselves up with harsh and critical judgments and endlessly lash out at our actor for our fears. Admit when you are afraid and the fear begins to soften. A slight turning over and seeing and writing out your accomplishments (both large and small) can go a long way toward encouraging the little toddler actor. I remember after that difficult show ended that I was being harsh and critical to everyone who stumbled across my path. That was nothing to the beating and slashing I was doing to myself. Nobody could do anything to help me. So what I needed to do was give myself some compassion. I had to love myself. Give yourself some credit, too. We fail to recognize how far we've come in a short amount of time.

This is all ego based. This is all grounded in panic and does not serve our little efforts. We are now on a path, a pilgrimage, a journey, an adventure, and we must now begin to pay more attention. Look at the signs guiding you, look at those who ambush you, even the weather of your own moods defines whether you succeed or not.

One of the other damaging evils we do to ourselves is compare and despair ourselves and our careers against other people. "Oh, look at her! She had connections! She was always the favorite! I'm not there yet!" We wail. Looking at them and putting them on a pedestal, we don't ask, "How did they do it?" or "What can I learn from them?" or "What would it take of me to get there?" or "What steps could I take?" No, we compare and despair. The "yet" is what to keep the focus on. Keep focused on your own through line. Keep your eyes on your own target. Keep your eyes open to your next direction. Don't get caught up in the now or what you immediately see. Look beyond it.

If we wait until the acting muse or gods sit on our shoulders and breathe inspiration into us, we might never get around to it. Acting has to be done consistently and practiced even when you sleep or slumber through the travails of living. Let me explain: Acting is difficult; not the process so much as what we attach to it. Acting has to take a priority someplace in your life. You have to let it in. Acting for so long in my life ran second place to everything else I had to do. So I learned to act in the middle of my life. I couldn't force myself to act, but I could coach myself and keep my eyes on the target. It took me a long time to take my dreams seriously enough to activate them. It was all fear. Fear of getting what I wanted. Fear of rejection. Fear of failure. Fear plain and simple. I had to become a rebel in my life. I had to revolt against all I had learned.

New acting habits and attitudes toward our new lives take time to solidify, and once they do, we begin to make great strides very quickly. What we are doing is removing old ways and replacing them with new healthy ones. We are after long endured healing not the quick fixes. This all takes time. Time we don't think we have but I say what else is there to do? Well, you could join the priesthood. Now, that sounds fun.

Acting is the cure. Acting is an act of love. When you have love, you can do anything. The power you contain is infinite. When we are acting, we are in touch with powers beyond our own limited human powers.

Pop Quiz

List five times when you've waited on someone or something.

List five things you are *still* waiting on.

List five times when waiting has served you.

These following "acting practice" rules might serve you here.

Do One Thing Each Day for Your Actor

This "one thing" can be small and not a big deal. Sometimes, we attach so much to our acting careers that we forget that it is fun. Watch out for when your ego or critic is telling you, "You're not doing enough!" (Can't you just hear that negative *growl?*) This is the part of you that wants instant results, instant fame, and ignores the little, tiny, tender baby steps. No high jumps are required when you first start acting. We often think in huge terms. "I have to mail out fifty thousand headshots in order to get into a film" or "I have to break onto the Warner lot or I have to sleep my way to the top."

So, at this point in the game, do *one* thing each day. It can be sending out an e-mail notice, it can be making a small video of a scene, going to the acting class, sending *one* headshot to an agent. If you take one action each day, in one year you will have taken 365 steps toward your dreams.

Don't Think . . .

"Don't think" is a way to get out of the "analytical" side of things. Overthinking leads to stagnation and discouragement. I was once conducting a workshop and an actress asked, "Am I doing this right?!" and I said, "Just being in this room is doing it right! Trust yourself!" We often want to see the results of our work too soon. Think of it as a garden you are planting. (Remember the task in week 1 to buy a houseplant?) You are watering those seeds with each task you accomplish in this course. This overanalysis of things creates much confusion and obstructs us from our organic and original ideas. Ideas that are creative are actually psychic and should be trusted. Acting is a risky business. Acting is fun. Acting is healing. We shut down the creative powers when we stop and "think about it." I like acting that is mindless, ruthless, and action-filled. Have fun and get out of you head.

"I Want" Monologue

I don't know why you expect so much. What more do you want? What else can I do? I'm here. I'm here with you. What else can I do that I'm not doing? What is it? I can't make it out. You don't tell me yet—you want. You want. But I don't know what it is that you want. What is it? Do you want it? Do you? You don't know what it is I'm talking about, do you? You don't, do you? And yet you sit there and you want, you want, you want. And I stand here, and I don't know what it is that you want. I stand here, don't I? At least I'm here. I'm here with you. Look? See? Your *(noun)* is here. Right here, see? Two arms, two legs, and only one head just like everybody else. Yet you want. I feel that tug in you. Where do you want me? What do you want of me? Backward and forward, you want! That's what you wanted? That's what you wanted? That's all you wanted. Cry? That's too easy. You can't get over of it that way. It's another trick to get me off track. I'm going to find out if it takes me the rest of my life. I'm going to find out what it is you want. Do you hear me? I'm going to find out if it takes me the rest of my life, the rest of my life.

The above monologue is to be used next week. Try to memorize it.

Tasks

1. *Imagine how your favorite actor would play the role.*

   Do the "I want" monologue one time as your favorite actor and then make notes for yourself. How did Tom Cruise play it? How did Bette Midler play it? How about James Dean? What did "they" bring to the character that was different?

   When you do this, you are avoiding the rote and normal (realistic) way of the material.

   Allow yourself to play with this tool.

   This is not a tool of imitation, but rather a way to get to parts of the character you haven't noticed before. If you try to read the lines like somebody else, you are removing you and your ego out of the part and expanding to new and possibly better ideas than you previously held.

2. *What type are you? What type of characters are you drawn to?* From your script reading, create an ongoing list of characters you would love to play.

3. *Archive: Select a monologue that you used to love to perform.* Dust it off and breathe life into it again. Have you discovered anything new about the material? Write about it. How has it changed? How

have you changed? Do you feel more connected to it or distant from it? Do you understand the material better?

4. *Catalog: Go back through your script reading and select a monologue and a scene.* Put them into a special notebook. You are consciously building your own personal portfolio or songbook. Add monologues and scenes to this book so you have a collection of material always on hand. (So when they say, "Show us what you got, kid," you have something instead of a blank stare!)

5. *Go to an audition.* Allow yourself to have fun and stay in the moment. Go in there and give it your best shot! If you blow it, don't panic. This is your practice shot. Take it all with a grain of salt. Write down in your notebook and not most especially what you felt (yes, it's valid to feel the joy, happiness, anticipation, loss, and the anger, "I could have done better . . ."). Note for yourself what you would change. Were you in it? Were you distracted? Be as honest as you can. This is your process.

6. *Buy yourself some "audition" clothes.* Buy things that you feel radiant in. Write about each article in your notebook. How do these clothes make you feel?

7. *List five things that you place before your acting.* Be as ruthless and honest as you can. (My job: "They will never let me off for an audition so I have to quit." My friends: "I can't let them down . . ." My money troubles: "I can't act until I pay my bills, balance my checkbook . . ." This is not an exercise in beating yourself up, but one in examination of how much we allow to get in our paths.

8. *Walking it out.* Walk out your monologue or scene. Let it unfold in your mind. I call this giving it to the universe or plotting with God. I walk out my scene to gain inspiration and insight. I ask questions "How would the character move?" "How does he talk?" In fact, I talk the lines out (it helps me to memorize them). I also listen as I walk for good ideas: "Do this! Try that!" You might wish to carry a tiny journal along and make notes to yourself.

Week 4: Check-in

1. How many days did you do your "I remembers . . ."? Are they difficult for you? Are you writing them from a character's point of view yet?
2. What script did you read? Have you begun to dream more about acting? What characters did you like? What didn't you like?
3. Are you remembering to put images in your notebook? By putting images in, we are visualizing our lives. Seeing is believing.
4. Have you noticed any synchronicity yet? What was it? (Did any acting opportunities come your way?)
5. Any other issues come up for you?

Week 5
Act 2, Scene 1

We have spent the first four weeks of this workbook dismantling our "blocks" and building a solid platform for our acting. Now, we will begin to use this platform to focus on scripts and scenes. The next four weeks will be devoted to "working" as an actor. The aim will be performing while remaining "unblocked," which can be challenging.

In the next few weeks, you're going to be doing a lot of scene and monologue "practice." If you're doing the course solo, just work on monologues until you find someone to "practice" with.

A little word about scene work:

In my workshops, I've seen it over and over actors who "show up" in class and try to get by. Acting practice says, "Show up and be prepared." It's the second half of that sentence that's a little more difficult to get. To be prepared means we have to make the commitment to our scene work. I tell students that whatever energy they bring to my class (or any class) is most likely the same energy they put into their acting. It's a mirror. Scene work is how you learn to act. Scene work and the preparation of that scene work require dedication and commitment. It does little good to bring a noncommitted energy ("I just picked the scene last night.") to your acting. Bring all you have to your acting. The most favored excuse is "I don't have time . . ." Would you tell that to an agent or a casting director? I hope not. I'm not pointing this out to point the finger, by the way, but to make a point. We do this to avoid our acting. We do this because we are afraid of what will happen when we commit to acting. Gently ask yourself and observe what energy you bring to your acting class. When I was in acting training, I would never have dared to show up for a class without my scene work prepared. I was afraid I'd get kicked out of class.

Remember while doing the work in the following chapters to keep up with your "I remembers . . ." and script reading. Here we go.

WEEK 5, ACT 2, SCENE 1

The Script

The actor is given a script. You have two things to work with to bring it to life: first, the words on the page and second, your body and soul. With those two ingredients you must create a believable performance. You must make each circumstance in the script come across on stage or film. Your job as an actor is to make it 100 percent believable.

Acting is telling the "truth" even when we are fabricating, fibbing, and lying. I think the truth is just staying in the moment and going after what the character wants. The want is the most important thing in the play just like it is in your own life. A script is just a heightened version of your life. *The Glass Menagerie* was Tennessee Williams's life pumped up and put on the stage. Now I'm speaking primarily about linear scripts. There are also scripts that are "abstract." These are truths after a tab of acid or eating peyote buttons. But even those must be played "real."

The script is the blueprint to the playhouse you are going to work in. Within the script are all the tools for you to build a strong, solid performance, but it all begins with understanding the words and the intention of the writer. Each script will have a unique code that you must decipher and translate into playable "actions." Also, each script will have a different "tone": comedy, sitcom, drama, movie, musical, commercial, voice-over, etc. The role of the actor is making it truthful. By using imagination and training you can create wonderful characters.

When one character wants one thing and another person wants something different, conflict is created, which is the whole point of theater, movies, and even sitcoms. If the enemies are going to fall madly in love by the end of the show, we have to see the obstacles, the barriers that stand between them. That's fun to watch.

We are creating and recreating the drama, the conflict. Always look, search, and find the drama in scripts. A script is characters involved in the throws of drama which has not yet been resolved. You cannot play the scene as if you already know what the outcome is. That is "indicating" or "playing the result."

Scene Exploration

Through your "script reading," you have seen at least four scripts. The actor must find the "world" of the script by reading it numerous times and looking for clues. I will read a script at least two times before I start to "memorize" it so I can find the "world." After you read the script, you go scene by scene looking for little pieces to connect yourself with the material. Here are some seeding "questions" to ask yourself about your specific scene to be fully explored in your notebook:

a) During what time period (current day, 1920s, BC, Victorian era, etc.) does the script take place?
b) Where (hotel lobby, bedroom, mansion, living room, etc.) does the scene take place ?
c) What city/town (country, castle, trailer park, NYC, etc.) does the scene take place?
d) What does my role (leading man, hot chick, goofy side kick, mother, lawyer, etc.) mean in the scene?

Where is the conflict? What does each of the characters want?

Inventory: What props or furniture is needed? Be specific.

Music: What is the tempo (waltz, rock and roll, ballad, orchestral, etc.) of the scene?

Now that you've done the general overview of the script, you narrow it down to your character. Below are a few questions to help you get specific about your character's desires.

Five Important Questions

1. Who am I? (How old am I?)
2. Where am I? (What time is it?)
3. What do I *WANT* from the other person?
4. How do I make the other person feel in order to get what I want?
5. What do I do when I get what I want or don't want?

These questions are and should be fun. Don't labor over these questions. Don't make acting hard into something you hate. Make it fun. If something silly and nonsense comes up for you, use it. Trust it. Acting is not linear; acting is a crazy quilt and you are to pull from any and all sources. When I am going over a play, I do this process for every scene the character is in. I find that a character is different in each and every scene. Try to see the beginning, middle, and end of your character's journey.

Annie Hall—An Exercise

The next tool I'll give you to practice with is called *Annie Hall*. In the movie *Annie Hall* (written, directed, and starring Woody Allen) Woody and his girlfriend are talking and their "true thoughts" are displayed in subtitles.

So when you are working on a scene, you can use this tool to help you gain insight into the subtext (what isn't being said, what's being thought and felt, and what is lurking beneath the surface of the dialogue). It's also good to use when working on interior monologue of a character.

The way to do it: You speak the lines as written, and as you go through the scene, you say out loud what the character is thinking . . . Talk over the other person's lines (this is not an exercise in being polite). This is a rehearsal, not a performance.

> *You must learn to trust who you are.*
> *There is no one else like you.*
> —Michael Shurtleff

Putting "Actions" to Work in Your Scene Work

When acting, you are dealing with small commitments to actions. The commitment to a specific action throws a lot of actors. It threw me because it was overintellectualized. Remember to "keep it simple." Choosing the language is important and private. The reason we enumerate on them in class is to share them. But you don't want the audience to know you are playing. Choose words that put a fire beneath you and charge you up. Don't pick boring, intellectual words. They must mean something to you. And if you can't think of the right action, don't be discouraged. Keep trying on words like trying on clothes for that oh, so important date ("that shirt, that dress, that hair style, that works, that looks stupid, that's fun. I look hot in that.") Write all your ideas down for the character, even the dumb ones. It's usually the silly ones that click for us.

As actors, we must continually choose an action and stick with it—a *specific* action. Action means motion. So often, we get stuck in the words, we lose sight that acting is a bold, bodily experience. Acting is character in motion. Acting is moving, doing, not only speaking. Even in the saying you are doing something. Make grand actions, make strong choices and commit to them. You can change your mind later, but always pick strong actions and stick to them.

I Want

Finish the following sentence as your character (pick a *strong* acting verb):

I want to_____
I want to_____
I want to_____
I want to_____
I want to_____

The action is the "Golden Key" to acting. What the character wants. Also it's good to look at what the character doesn't want. Amanda in *The Glass Menagerie* does *not* want her son to be a drunk and her daughter to be an old maid. This points her to what she does want: Tom to be responsible and Laura to find a good man. This can help you discover what they want. The want also has to have a specific person it's being acted upon. (e.g., Amanda: "I want to enroll Tom into finding Laura a husband!") You can tell if it is accomplished or not. You can constantly tell if you're winning or losing. Think of it in terms of your own life. You want to act, so you come to class. You want to eat, so you cook dinner. You want to book a part, so you go to auditions. Actors tend to disregard the fact that characters in plays are just like us. They want what we want on some level!

When we act, we take the ordinary details of life, and transfer them onto the stage. The moment we put it on stage, it grows larger. Acting is not life, not "real" life. Acting is larger than life. In certain traditions and styles, we are taught that acting is just the same as living. That has not been my experience. A rule I devised for myself is "never be boring!" Acting can have no energy behind it if we think of it in terms of real life because we'll dampen and limit our choices. Acting is best when it is sharp, crisp, and full of life. If I had to live out my life on stage, that would bore me to tears. I like acting for the fact that I get to play a character other than myself.

Assuming the Role

I build characters from the outside in. Give me a chipped tooth, a limp and with that the rest comes.
—Carol Burnett

You must believe that *you are* the role. You must assume you are the character. Start immediately to build the character with the words "I am" and "I want." This helps us find ourselves in the role. If we jump with both feet into the character, we are halfway there. "I am Blanche . . ." "I am Stanley . . ." "I am Treplev . . ." "I am Bette Davis . . ." No matter what character you are playing, start speaking the character through the words "I" not "him" or "her," because when you do, you take ownership of the role and the character and you become merged as one. In improv, they teach to say "yes" to everything. I like this. It's a good idea to bond instantly with the character. I've seen many great actors give up because they create a gulf between themselves and the character. "I'm not like that!" or "I would never do that!" instead of assuming since the writer intended the character to do it, it is right.

First flashes of a character are *very* important. I've learned that these first impulses are usually right on target. I connect with these first images I have of the character (what I see in my mind's eye as I read the script). I try to visualize the character more than "think" about him. I think of these early flashes as "coming attractions" to the actual character I'll eventually create. I write these insights down and later act on them. I get my imagination heated up with these first impressions.

Acting is a bodily activity. When I am creating a character, I take a lot of walks. I fiddle with the magical "what if" instead of "why." I try to maintain a sense of play with my characters.

When I first read the role of Davis Davis in *Off Hollywood* and it said in the character description "Davis is a poor man's Orson Welles," I knew *how* to play him. The other key was "Davis sticks out like a sore thumb." It's not rational, but I *knew* I could act that. This gave me one of the keys to how this character would look, think, and act. I wrote those notes down in the margins of my script. In fact, I showed up at the rehearsal dresses as the character. I wore a vintage, wool flight jacket, suspenders, a tie from the 1930s, and a pair of vintage, tweed pants and dress shoes.

Character Study

Exploration Questions:

Who am I?
Who are the other characters?
What is the relationship (lovers, enemies, family, etc.) between the characters?
What color is the character?
How does the character dress (evening gown, suit, swim trunks, etc.)?
What are the circumstances of the character's life?

Write a character biography (include numerous "I wants . . .")
What are the character's dreams?

Build and fashion the character how the character looks.
How does the character dress? What is their hairstyle?

How do others in the play react (or say) to your character?
How does the character walk, talk, run, dance, and sing?

How do you relate to the character? What do you have in common? Do you like the character?

Connect the dots. (How does the character connect to you?) What do you have in common? Don't think about what you don't have. Think about what you do have.

Acting is basically building, playing, pulling, and attracting the right things for the part. Acting does not have to be murderous and torturous. We each have our own unique style of acting. Acting is as individual as the person. There are a million different approaches or methods to acting.

In acting, we want to see the character struggle, rise above circumstances, *not* the actor. It's the playwright and the character we have to fight for; it's not ourselves that we play, but the larger part of ourselves or the "character" side of ourselves. We must learn to develop that character.

The piece you play in a script is an interesting way to look at the character. You can objectively examine and experiment with your placement in the play. You can be a puzzle piece. "I am the leading man." "I am the funny old bag . . ." "I am the ingenue." We should work with archetypes or stereotypes we are told to avoid. I know this is bold, but speaking about the character in larger than life terms, we can then narrow in on the specifics. Now you don't just play "nurse" or "lover," you begin with broad ideas and make them more specific in the rehearsal process.

Do you like the scene you are playing? If you don't, find one that you do enjoy. You are never tied to do anything in this workshop. What text do you love or hate? (If you feel strongly one way or the other about a certain line or phrase, that can indicate where your passion is.)

Commitment to Character

Investment requires responsibility. Responsibility requests that we respect our acting talents. Respect is born out of generosity and a lighthearted approach. I'm not suggesting that acting is by any stretch an easy arena to enter into. We don't give ourselves permission to act badly. By that, I'm not saying be lazy and not extend effort into your craft, but with keeping it simple removes us from the emergency: "I got to get it done now. I have to be perfect." You can allow your acting career to evolve and alter as you change. Acting does require tenacity, but shaming and guilting our little actor does no good. Forgiveness and love are the keys to unblocking the frightened actor.

> *Very often a risk is worth taking simply*
> *for the sake of taking it.*
> —Julia Cameron

Acting is a series of beginnings. Where do you start? You start wherever you are to build your acting career. The challenge to acting is resiliency. We begin afresh each time we approach a character or a play. We must be like clay or blank canvas and be easily molded when we act. To me acting is very much like collecting—an image of this, a part of that; a song lyric to get that emotion across; that shoe, these colors. When we stay in the question of "what would it take to bring this character to life?" we are in the position of finding the solutions or being presented with them in strange yet perfect ways. "Oh, what my uncle said to me when I was sixteen is how angry this character is."

> *What an actor must look for in a*
> *play is something important.*
> —Michael Shurtleff

Each character has a prescription—a code that the actor is trying to break. Some characters are deep and require lots of in-depth study and some are more shallow. That's okay. Each character I put on stage is a combination of all I've learned. This doesn't mean that I don't care and am not connected or committed, it's just I've learned to let the character work through me. I do what the character wants. Each role requires different powers. If I'm engaged in a light comedy, I digest comedy, I dive into other comedians. I listen to and watch Bette Midler, Robin Williams, or Whoopi Goldberg. If I'm playing a more serious role, I usually listen to lots of song to put me in the mood. I remember I was doing a scene from *Safe Sex* where the character is still in mourning over his dead lover. I listened to Karen Carpenter's version of "Ticket to Ride" over and over again.

We imitate the boss. We mock a friend. We sing along to the radio. We rehearse in the showers. We have an endless supply of characters cued up waiting for us to show them the light. But they are usually hiding, lurking around in the dark. When we were children, it was easy to do as we played "make believe," but as adults, we "think" about character. I say don't think. Become irrational, emotional, and creative again. Play with your characters. Even if the character we are working on is like us, it never is us. We are playing a higher level of ourselves. How do you create a character? Do you do it from the bottom-up or the top-down? I've done it all ways. Each character you play will requires different energies and you'll draw from different sources available. You might begin with a costume to help get you in the mood or a pair of shoes. By consciously examining how we unearth and build our characters, we maintain a sense of fun instead of a sense of fear and dread.

Where Does the Character Live?

Where does the character live inside of you? Where does he or she reside? What muscles, voice, teeth, and hair does the character take of you? What is the physical space for the character? Give him some room and don't be stingy. What part of your personality, personae, and character does your character come from? Which ideas and principles do you bring to the part? What part of the body? You must know where inside of you the character resides. You must faithfully go there each time. The character is never far removed from you. Never put a gulf between you and the character. Think instead of all the things you have in common with that character and build it from there.

What part of the body do you move in order to arrive at the character? Where does the character take you? You must know the truth of the character and nothing can be faked. I also say that you must immediately grow into the character. Don't create a separation. Create exciting characters by tapping into the infinite well that you have. When you already believe you are the character, you will be that character. Trust that your work is believable. Trust your hunches. Trust your ideas.

Trust your intuition. They are there to help you build the character. Be inspired through your body. Trust the spirit of the character. I'm not saying that if you are playing a murderer that you obtain a machine gun. What I am saying is look deep within you for areas where you have wanted to kill, or murder some person, place, or thing. Let God work through you. Let yourself be guided to the character.

Another good way to establish ourselves in the character is to write our "I remembers . . ." from the characters' viewpoint. Do this at least three times this week.

When playing a character that is close to you, don't strain. I find these are the hardest to do because we have a tendency to overact. We have to prove we are "acting" instead of keeping it simple. "I don't know what I'm doing with this character! I feel like I'm just saying a bunch of lines!" an exasperated student exclaimed to me during a workshop when he as playing Tom from *The Glass Menagerie*, a character really close to his own personality.

Avoid overthinking your character to death.

When I act, I don't discount anything. I try to use everything (including the kitchen sink) in my rendering of characters. Often, when creating a character, I start with the speech pattern. I used to *hate* the sound of my "high-pitched" voice until I learned it was my strongest calling card. I start with asking myself, "Do they have a speech impediment or funny language pattern? Where does their voice come from?" I then go to the feet (the soul of the character!) and concentrate on what shoes they wear. I'm always very specific about this. The way a character will move determines their energy. I then begin to find costume pieces. No, I don't wait for the costume designer. I like to get a head start. "I can play any character if I have the right shoes," Bette Midler once said. The costume is very important to me. I then write about the character (from the "five questions").

Can you somehow connect with their voice? Is the voice for the character different than yours? If the character has a distinct "problem" with their voice or a certain pattern of words, I use that as a jumping off point. No character I play has exactly the same voice as mine. I try to make each one have some quirk about their voice. And don't think just because I do something, it will work for you. All actors are uniquely different, and different tools will inspire them in different ways.

I also do a writing based on metaphor. This is one I did for the character Bomber in *Picnic*: "I am a butterfly. I am a Southern dive-bombing moth. I am a baseball bat. I am a four-alarm fire." I then begin to imagine the surroundings and circumstances and the time period. All this time, I use the magic words: "Act as if . . ." This immediately puts me into another frame of mind in which to create. And one of the most important things I do is walk for ideas. I like to walk just around the time the sun begins to go down and the sky starts to become blue-black. I walk in order to collect inner images of how the character thinks, acts, and does. I walk to get both sides of the brain to harmonize together.

When I am putting together a character, it has become a habit with me that I surround myself with images of the character. Photos of what they might look like, clothes they might wear, places they live, cars they drive, social circle, etc. I tend to read books they would read or watch movies they would watch. If I'm playing a comedy, I tend to watch old comedies and listen to Bette Midler a whole lot. I have always thought of acting much like cooking a good meal. You add a dash of this, a whole lot of that, and a pinch of those until the character is cooked. For me, the characters all begin inside my mind. And then the character manifests itself on the outside. This is my way. Yours may be very different.

How do you create characters? Do you do it from the outside in or the inside out? There are no wrong ways to develop characters. Do you yourself have character? Are you charming, selfish, a dreamer, or a bully? Do you have an obnoxious voice? What separates you from the other animals in the acting zoo? If you can't think of anything, go back over your "vein of gold" list from week 1. As Martha Graham advises us, "Because there is only one of you in all time, this expression is unique . . ." Often, it's the personality traits that you don't like that makes you an interesting character. Acting is about generating what we are and putting that expression onto the stage. If you're telling yourself you are boring, then you probably need to develop some character.

Observations

If you go deeply in one thing, you know everything else.
—Natalie Goldberg

When you watch scene work, it is essential that you notice what is "hot" in the scene. What do I mean by that? What is alive and awake in the scene? In other words, where was the work "present"? When you tell someone about their work, don't say "It was okay . . ." or "I felt you should . . ." or "It was great." We don't have to label the work. This doesn't give them much information. Instead say, "I remember the moment you said or did . . ." Give your acting peers *specific* details about what they did. Acting is not only paying attention to what we do but what others do. The more honed your mind is to watching others, the more alive, awake, and interesting your acting will be. I'll give you an example. I recently did a series of one-act plays. I was in the first one of the evening and not in the second one, so I got to scurry out of my costume during intermission and sit and watch the second show. There was a woman who fascinated me. Every night, she sang a song and did this rope motion with her hand and this little country dance as she mimicked *The Best Little Whorehouse in Texas*. I could recall the movement because it was so specific. Watching others and witnessing what they do is another missed chance in acting.

Above all, if you can't recall what someone does, don't worry about it. You are learning to watch and listen. Over time, you'll get better at it, just something to think about.

Audition Blues

Last week, I asked you to go on an audition. Did you do it? Did you not find the time? Did you show up and leave? Did you show up, kick ass, and take names? Did you throw up? If you didn't go, ask yourself in a very nonjudgmental way, "What stopped me?" And be very gentle when you answer. Try to go on one next week. Whatever you did was right for you and will give you a clue to where you might still be blocked.

I still have to audition. Unfortunately, I must face this terrifying spectrum as well. No one is exempt from auditions. I wish I could spare you this process, but it is part of the business of being an actor. In order to act, we must face the terrible auditions. I actually had to make friends with this very intimidating monster. To stand in a room or a stage so uncertain, not sure if they want you is horrific. I don't know a single actor who likes this procedure. It's hard to not feel like a piece of meat, knowing that they might not want me and yet they hold my destiny in their hands. It took me time to learn that the only thing I had to give was myself and my talent. I had to release the drama of the audition. How did I ever do it? Well, I used whatever drama I felt and put that emotion into the material I was working on. If I felt particularly pressured by the casting director, I put that into what I showed them. That worked better than ignoring what I really felt . . . I also tried to make the audition a game as much as possible. There are a million little tricks the actor will learn, but you only learn them by "going" to auditions.

Some auditions go great. Some complete dog poop. But if you just keep in the spirit of "what did I learn?" they won't burn you out. Treat each audition like a class. My friend recently said to me after he had gone on an audition he didn't "feel" secure about. We would fare better if we viewed each audition like a class where we can learn from each one. This is not to say we don't feel our disappointment. But we don't stop too long to examine and reexamine. But the fact is if you keep auditioning, you get better, but if you stop, you get rusty. When you look at your audition, look at it from your most gentle and tender side. Ask, "What can I improve?" not "What did I do wrong?"

We often over criticize and critique our auditions. We pick them apart and tear ourselves down with "would of, could of, and should of . . ." thinking. What is needed from us is admitting our courage in showing up. As actors, we need to congratulate ourselves for every action we take. Each audition is one step closer. And the thing about taking steps is you can only do one at a time. You can't get to the top of a staircase without walking up it. Acting is no different. Even on your worst days, when you feel pitiful and ashamed and like no one in the world cares if you ever act again, just remind yourself that your time will come again if you just continue to take actions.

I remember when I used to stall out after auditions. I couldn't go on with the rest of my life! I had to call and fret with friends about it. I had to phone people up and tell them how rich I was going to be when the series was going to take off when I only had a callback. I had to cavil, complain, and champion instead of taking it in stride and moving on to the next thing. This had to change. Now, I'm ambitious in a gentle way. I don't have to drag myself over the coals to make it happen. My soul knows more than I do.

I also used to go into the casting director's office with a huge chip (resentments) on my shoulders. I had to drop that as well. I had to think of them as friends to my career. I became less anxious (I learned how to use it!) and replaced negativity with positive thoughts—remember, the casting directors have called you in because they want to "see" you. They want you to win. Now, I'm not saying that we get every audition (yes, my heart still breaks when the part goes to someone else, someone with less talent my ego *always* pouts. But not as much as it used to), but we bless and thank them for the opportunity (think of all the poor actors who aren't auditioning) and move on quickly to the next right action. I also changed my "viewpoint" of my agent and start praising them instead of being *another* complaining (pain in the ass) actor! I had to get myself working before my agent did! I started by being *happy* at every audition! If it was for a midget audition, if it was for an elf, a leprechaun, or a lawn gnome, I just went in with a great attitude (knowing I most likely would not get cast) and just played and had fun, and in little over a month of this "new way," I booked a commercial spot that has paid me over $10,000.

Auditions seem to come to me when I'm the most "busy," when I have a lot going on. I used to get all dramatic and over the top and wail, "Oh god! I have an audition!" as the wheels spun me out of control, thinking how I'd have to give up my entire life for one audition. Auditions are a part of the actor's life. Auditions should not be looked at as gruesome burdens but as another chance to practice. We give them too much weight. Don't get tossed because you have an audition. Go to it, do your work, and then go on with your life.

Auditions are so unpredictable that I had to disassociate myself with the end result. I had to trust that I always did a great job. There was a point that I would buy myself an ice cream cone after auditions just for showing up.

On the days when we think our audition is great, we don't get called back. On the occasions when we think it's rotten and we should sell flowers instead, well, we get the part. So a rule of thumb that I developed is, give my all at every audition and walk out proud and let the universe do the rest.

Sometimes, we'll go to an audition and it won't go. We've done our work, we've shown up prepared, but we get before the camera or on the stage and we flop—this is necessary. We could use this as an exercise in self-torture, ridicule, and blame and stop. Don't stop! Find a quiet place, sit down, and breathe (crying is okay)—let the audition slip away from you. Imagine it leaving you. Imagine it going back into the universe and see another two doors opening for you. Remember acting practice is mostly about showing up. We sometimes do a *"bad"* audition. Before, we would allow that to hinder our progress, no longer. This is the moment you must show up for yourself. Show up first at the page. Write about that terrible audition. Write whatever comes up for you no matter how trivial you think it is. Did you get taken out by anger? What threw you off center?

Example: "God, I ate that one! They ate lunch during my monologue! I could feel my hand tremble . . . the paper shook. I did come up with a funny improv line which they didn't get. I could only hear the fat guy munching on a pickle . . . I hated the director. She didn't like me at all."

Write fast and don't think. This is not an analysis tool. Be petty. Write at what makes you angry. Get all the hurts on the page. Now, tell them who you are. Tell them why you are going to succeed. Tell them your plans. Write affirmations. Write a quick action plan of what you are committed to doing. Do one thing.

This has been a lot to take it, I'll admit it. Go have a treat of some kind. A walk, a night on the town, a cup of coffee, a bike ride, get a haircut . . . You deserve it.

Tasks

1. *Where does the character live in you?* Write out the things within you that you change to create the character (my voice, my hair, my hand movements, etc.).

2. *Examine your environment.* Start with the sentence, "Where am I . . ." and go for fifteen minutes.

   Example: "Where am I? I'm at my makeshift writing desk. A desk made of milk crates and a door that was left behind by the previous owners of the apartment before I moved in. The walls are painted Curious George yellow. I'm in Los Angeles, Hollywood to me, where film rules the world. Everyone is connected to films in this town. I'm burning incense."

3. *Make a list of all the "methods" of acting you've tried.* What did you learn? Did you ever get caught up in the teacher or group or politics and forget you wanted to act? Write a little about what the experience did for you.

4. *Character: How do you create a character?* Be specific.

5. *Write an "I remember . . ."* At all the ages from the characters' point of view.

6. *"Circle game."* Grab a chair, put it in the center of the room, and walk around and around it while you think about your character. Add a "layer" each time you circle. If you're doing this with another actor, have them "build a character" on you! Sit down in the chair and read your "I want" monologue as that character! This is a *very*

good way to "get in character" while at auditions or on the set or backstage!

7. *Perform a monologue from your "play reading."*

8. *Assemble a costume plot for your character.* Make each article of clothing have a history. Where did the character obtain each article of clothing? Be specific!

9. *Go shopping for your character.* Buy your characters wardrobe. I like to do this early in the process so I can start to feel the character through clothes!

10. *Stay "in" and write an "I remember . . ." about five people you know.* Do this quick and write with specific details. Their hair, their voice, their habits, etc.

11. *Go "out" and observe five people and write a character description.* Write about their clothes, their hair, what do they want, what do they burn for, and what are their dreams?

12. *Actions: List twenty things you could do in your scene.* (Eat, tie shoes, sort mail) Pick five and do them in the scene (even if briefly). The next time you do the scene, pick five more.

13. *When you read your next script, begin to jot down things the character's wants.*

Week 5: Check-in

1. How many days did you do your "I remembers . . ."? Are they difficult for you? Are you writing them from a character's point of view yet?
2. What script did you read? Are you finding you like a certain style of script? Have you begun to take note of the circumstances, props, and costumes as you read?
3. Are you remembering to put images in your notebook? By putting images in, we are visualizing our lives. Seeing is believing.

4. Have you noticed any synchronicity yet? What was it? (Did any acting opportunities come your way?)
5. Any other issues come up for you?

Note: How did your audition go? Please write about it. What would you change? What did you like? At this point, you should try to go on one audition a week. This is good practice.

Week 6
Act 2, Scene 2

"Money Makes the World Go Round!"

This week we will start to examine a topic that "blocks" a lot of actors: *Money!* I say we will start to examine it, look at it, and play with it because it's a real high-voltage topic for a lot of us. We think we have to "make a living" acting. We think we have to make a million dollars a week on a series or we think we need to be "broke" to be an actor. But I want to say, "You already are rich!" You are rich because you have a unique gift and no one else in the universe is exactly like you. Now all you need to create a "business" around your acting is: some good headshots, a demo reel, and a little drive.

> *Riches do not respond to wishes. They respond only*
> *to definite plans, backed by definite desires,*
> *through constant persistence.*
> —Napoleon Hill

You can get paid acting as soon as you start telling the universe that you'd like to. I know this will sound like a lot of bunk to those who are working day jobs and not earning a living from your acting. But we're talking about building your finances through acting one step at a time. Sometimes, we need to look at our "money" believes and discard some of the negative ones. My stepdad told me when I first started to act, "You'll never make money acting!" I bought into this for many years and *did not* make any money from it, but many years later, I have the paycheck stubs to prove that I did make money acting.

I'm going to be discussing some concepts and terms that at first might make you balk and throw a temper tantrum and quit. Please understand that I have been in your shoes. I have been broke. I have been in the situation of not having enough money to pay my rent, but once I started to understand my relationship with money (and acting) things began to *slowly* change for me. So let's not expect of ourselves to undo this in one essay. The following concepts I'm going to give you are "tools" to work on your prosperity.

"Time is money and the money is mine!" Madonna (multimillionaire) is said to have quipped early in her career. I agree with her. We often squander our time and our money on things that have little or *nothing* to do with our careers as actors. This can be very challenging to face, but stick with me. I have noticed students who are constantly late usually have "money" problems. They always seem to be "behind" in paying their bills, behind the clock, and behind the checkbook. I suggest if you want to make money, clean up your "time" issues. Give yourself plenty of time and you'll start to see a shift in your pocketbook.

Actors are also tempted by a bunch of expensive headshots, courses, "casting director," and "agent" workshops. These can be good, but they can also drain the bank account if you are not careful. Part of your "job" as an actor is to get hired to work on acting jobs, but you don't need to spend thousands of dollars to do it! Keep in mind that you are operating a "business" and what you do with your money counts.

We must understand that it is *our* time and *our* money and we can spend it however we please. Ask yourself, "Are those $300 tickets to the Lady Gaga concert going to help my career?" If it is going to inspire you, sure, but if you can spend those dollars toward furthering your own career, use it there, and the same with going to movies, buying CDs, books, clothes, and expensive dinners. Always ask, "Am I making the smartest choice with my money and my time?!"

The next part of making money is seeing it expand. I once did a consultation with Viki King (author of *How to Write a Movie in 21 Days*), and she taught me the "law of ten" game. I'm going to share it with you. When you get a check (from acting or your day job), multiply the amount by ten and imagine you are depositing that amount in your checking account. For example, you get a residual check for $500. Multiply it by ten and imagine you are depositing $5,000 in the bank. This is a wonderful tool and has really helped me increase my income.

I have also expanded the game: I multiply everything I spend by ten and see that money coming *back* to me. If I spend $20 on gas, I multiply that amount by ten and say to myself, "Two hundred dollars are now coming back to me in wonderful, unexpected ways!" I also take 10 percent out of each check and put it into a savings account. That way I'm giving something back to myself in the form of savings.

I know a lot of this above metaphysical, New Age stuff might seem like crap to you, but all I'm suggesting is, you play with the concepts. When I first started to study metaphysical concepts at the Church of Religious Science, I had horrible believes about money, and over the years, I've learned to make money acting. I also suggest a book by Napoleon Hill called *Think and Grow Rich*. In this book, he talks about organizing a plan in which to make money. You can do the same thing with your acting career.

I'll also list some of my favorite "money" affirmations for you to use. You might pick one and say it out loud each day with "feeling" and you might start to see a shift in your finances. These are the following money affirmations:

1. My income is constantly increasing.
2. Checks and more checks are mine.
3. I now accept great pay to play great parts.
4. I am a rich and successful actor.
5. I *deserve* to make money acting.

Now that we've put that big "block" on the table, I mentioned early on in this chapter that you are already "rich." You are rich with the body of work that you have been amassing. Writing your daily "I remembers . . ." has given you a body of your own stories that can be utilized for acting material. You have also been beefing up on scripts through your weekly reading. See, there is a never-ending catalog or database of material for you to work on.

This week I want you to read your "I remembers . . ." and create a monologue from them. Here is one that I created from mine.

(Dick walks through the office, speaking in a loud voice carrying the junk from his recently cleaned out desk.)

Dick: I wanted to say good-bye to you all! It was so much fun working here—answering your phones, sorting your mail, and making coffee for you all! Thank you for the peanuts you paid me! I am so thankful I had time to work on my own scripts! I only wish I had done less. I only wish I had stolen more office supplies. I only wish I had made *more* copies on your copier, but, alas, my good people, we must part.

(Finally, Dick arrives at his bosses' office and slings open the door and the boss is in the middle of a pow-wow with some "bigwigs" from NYC.)

Dick: Chief, I just wanted to say, what a distinct pleasure it was working for you and putting another toupee on your head!

(The boss touches his hair by instinct.)

Dick: That's right, I said toupee! Come off it, everyone knows it's a rug!

This scene is taken from a screenplay called *Pyramid Scheme* that I wrote from my "I remembers . . ." I had enough material to organize it into a script. (One of the tasks this week is to create a monologue from your "I remembers . . .") Please don't skip this very fun tool.

Danger!

Piece by piece, working out the vision night and day.
All it takes is time and perseverance.
With a little luck along the way.
—Stephen Sondheim

When we use our acting, we feel useful to the world. We become actually attractive, and we attract acting parts to us. The more we engage in acting practice, the more God acts in our behalf. We see more things as helping us out. The less rigid we become. We seem to need less from the outside world as we know our acting is what really matters.

It's actually a matter of balance when we find we are being road tested by life, by God. We are tempted to stop, to abandon our acting practice, but remember the rule "Never give up!" It's the acting against the odds that gives us strength and shape. It's been my experience that I grow more when I'm acting, when I'm not in the mood, not feeling like it or not feeling well.

At six weeks, I think this is a turning point: It's good to stop here on this part of the path and take a quick check at the ground we've covered.

Look at the pieces of yourself that you've recovered and discovered. Even when you feel sad, discouraged, and outraged, don't you have hope biting at your heels? "Hey, I am too an actor!" We find ourselves yelling.

We are tempted by our tempers—temporary flashes of thunder that illuminates the evolving soul. Our true selves are *awakening*. Without this time to take an inventory, we might lose sight of the heights we've actually accomplished. The "I remembers . . ." and script readings have given you a firm foundation upon which you can now trust. On the worst days, you do them out of obligation and duty because I tell you to, but remember they will keep you grounded during the passing storm.

We might be in the predicament of: "I really have wanted to act, but have not acted. Or I do need a better agent or I haven't taken the chance to call my agent. I've been mad . . ." We find ourselves wanting to take action, ready to take a risk, but . . .

But we *still* have fears. Now is a good time to notice what actions you falter on because of fear. We don't know where God is leading us. We don't know where our next break will come from. How can we know such things? That's the surprise of acting. One day nothing and then the door suddenly opens up. We get a phone call. We are cast in the film. Our friend has written a part for us. The only things we can know for certain is: "Did I practice today?" "Have I put my headshots out into the world or are they sitting in a box on the shelf?"

> *The truth is that we are meant to be bountiful and live.*
> —Julia Cameron

Our next break is up to God, not us. "Faith without works is dead," the old slogan tells us. And as actors, our work is making sure we are responsible for our doable actions. "Have I returned phone calls?" "Have I rehearsed my scene?" "Have I submitted myself?" "Did I read the new script my agent sent me?"

Yes, we might be quaking in our boots, shaking with fears and doubts, but remember Nancy Sinatra's mantra: "These boots are made for walking" and keep walking. When you feel depressed (repression), get out of the house, grab a stack of postcards, and mail them out to agents or casting directors. Call a supportive friend or loved one, dance around to Madonna . . . Do anything but quit. "A winner *never* quits and a quitter *never* wins!" Napoleon Hill author of *Think and Grow Rich* reminds us.

Now is not the time to stop and criticize yourself. Now is the time to keep yourself in flight. Now is the time to go to those rehearsals, those auditions, to show up even if your heart breaks. Any actor will assure you that sometimes we do great work when we are not in the right mood.

We have leaped and the net still isn't certain. It might be curtains any minute for our acting careers. But we continue to show up. We daily gain stamina by engaging in the next doable action. Fear is something that tempts us all to stop and stall. This time, don't give up. Mail out postcards (one a day even), get new headshots, read a script, or call your agent. Remember, "Actions speak louder than words."

If all this sounds dangerous to you, good. I want you to feel challenged and inspired. It's a good idea to obtain a sense of danger to your acting. This danger is actually the fire for your desire. Often, we feel as if we're going to get consumed by our passion to act—like being swallowed up in a vacuum cleaner hose—the world will contain and sustain your desires to act. Trust it by showing it you're doing your actions.

"Fake it till you make it." I love this expression because it tells to act like we have all the talent and success until we actually have it. It also ties in to "Act as if . . . ," which means you act like or pretend or visualize *what* you want to be and go about your life as if you have it already. This requires some definite thinking because in the end it is all up to us. We determine the success we have. This means that we have to look at some of our thought and action patterns. This is not good news for most of us who live our lives on automatic pilot or who stumble along following what others want us to do. It means we need to take a stand in our lives.

Walking It Out

Walk out your monologue or scene. Let it unfold in your mind. I call this giving it to the universe or plotting with God. I walk out my scene to gain inspiration and insight. I ask questions: "How would the character move?" "How does he talk?" In fact, I talk the lines out (it helps me to memorize them). I also listen as I walk for good ideas "Do this! Try that!" You might wish to carry a tiny journal along and make notes to yourself.

I was rehearsing for a show called *The Eight: The Reindeer Monologues* and found it very difficult to learn Cupid's entire monologue (five pages!) through my ordinary methods of memorizing it by rote and rehearsing it, so I tried another tactic that worked for me. I would go on walks in the mornings while running the entire monologue out loud over and over again. Not only did I get all the lines memorized, but while I was walking I had flashes of what the character would wear, the music for my entrance and even his sinister laugh.

The Rejection Factor

Live past the moment. Get past it, don't give up, hang on till the valuable books show up and the Oscar and doctorates and people's love pour in.
—Ruth Gordon

"Rejection is God's way of protecting you," a friend of mine said. "No, no, and *no!*" Get used to hearing that word. Risk is tied to the word "no." But don't listen to the "no." What I mean by this is don't take it personally. Don't let it toss you away. People (some of them very close to you) will say "No." Don't be phased by it. They don't know. The casting directors will tell you "No." Agents will tell you "No." You'll get the cold rejection letter in the mail. You won't hear anything at all after auditioning nine times. We're all adults and we know that nobody can really tell us "no," but as toddler actors we tend to get thrown off course by it. Of course, we do. We aren't taught that one door closes and another opens if you keep knocking. Sometimes, this takes incredible amounts of strength and courage, but it must be our new way.

Think of it this way: If you're hearing "no," that's a good indication that a break is about to come *if* we keep moving, keep dancing, keep practicing, and keep trying. The rub is to remain committed to our daily actions. Stay on the path and remain sure your miracle is just out of sight. Don't hover by the phone, steeping in anxiety. Get out of the house and have some fun, and the waited for phone call will come. Keep yourself in circulation. I once heard that a very famous poet wallpapered his bathroom with rejection letters from places that refused to publish his work. How many "nos" have you heard lately? Make a list of your rejections. Wear them like badges of honor.

Entrances

Cause excitement when you make an entrance. Create a flurry. When I watch a film or a play, I look for the actors who make dramatic entrances. I enjoy creating my entrances. I like to enhance or enchant the audience to engage in the life of the character. Make grand entrances. Don't be boring. Make your character come full throttle onstage. Come on stage or on camera with something interesting. This is where the moment before is so important to play with. Where are you coming from (*be specific!*)? How did you get there (walked, rode on horseback, spaceship, subway, up a flight of stairs)?

In essence, you are announcing your character when you make an entrance. You carry their "baggage" with you. You can say so many things about the character before you even utter your first sentence. I like an entrance that is alive, that has passion, and that is clever and clear. Each part of a script can be broken down scene by scent to find an "entrance." Mozart in *Amadeus* makes a different entrance in the scene where he's going to meet the Emperor Joseph and the royal court than he does in the scene when he's drunk at a party later in the script. Each scene must begin with a different organic entrance.

The entrance is one of the most important (and overlooked) elements of the character building process. It can be one of the most creative and challenging. Uta Hagen talks about them in her book *Respect for Acting*. When I read that chapter, it gave me the keys to a special kingdom of acting. After that, I tried to make entrances my specialty. I never know exactly how I'm going to enter, but I have a whole bunch of things lined up. (I'll tell you a secret: I never do the same one twice!) There are many ways to make an entrance. I urge you to practice or play with this tool. Over the next week, watch yourself and others who makes good entrances? And who just stands on stage "waiting" for their lines?

WEEK 6, ACT 2, SCENE 2

Character Soundtrack

I was recently driving in the car with a friend, and she played the Trisha Yearwood song "The Song Remembers When" and it moved me to tears. The song was about a woman who had a romance that went sour and she hears a song on the radio and she thinks about the long-ago lover. I use music constantly when I create my character. I'm not a singer (although when I live another life, I'd like to have a voice like Karen Carpenter), but music has always touched my nerves and moved me.

When you are assembling your notes for your character, don't overlook music! What is their theme song? What music do they sing along to? None. Maybe that says something about the character. "Hooray for Hollywood" was Davis Davis in *Off Hollywood*. When I was working on the film *Off Hollywood,* I used Patty Griffith's "Long Ride Home" as a way to get me in the mood to play my "overemotional" character. Something about the strum of the guitar and her woeful voice brought me to the rawness of myself. If anyone sees me before a show, I'm usually listing to music in my iPod for two reasons: first, to drown everyone out, and second, to center and focus myself.

For *The Reindeer Monologues* I chose "Dancing Queen" to make my entrance, and the whole audience broke up in laughter as I came prancing out with my pink antlers. It said everything about my character before I even opened my mouth. Years later, I used the same music when I entered the arena of stand-up comedy, and I swear it "won" the audiences for me as I wasn't coming out "cold turkey." I was working on a character from *Safe Sex,* and the character was mourning the loss of his lover and so I used the Carpenter's "Ticket to Ride" to get in the emotional state. Music has a profound "spiritual" factor and can trigger "memories" for us as it travels around the intellect.

When I create a character, I find different songs to underscore the character's emotions or mood. Music is very sensory. We feel music. Music makes us cry and laugh; it moves us. Is the character you're creating Mozart, Madonna, Judy Garland, Bette Midler, or Bruce Springsteen? Which song particularly fits for you? Finding the right music can inspire you to reach depths and heights you might not have dreamed of before. Is your character classical or rock and roll? You decide. This is a very private exercise I simply ask you to try this tool.

The day I got cast in the movie *Off Hollywood* I had an urge to buy Queen's "We Are the Champions," and I got the call that same night.

So write a quick list of songs that "move" you into the character you are playing. Now make a list of songs that "move" you personally.

Creating the *Right* Costume

One of my favorite holidays is Halloween. I love becoming someone else, slipping into a new skin. I believe that's how simple acting can and should be. It should be at least that much fun. That's how I began to act. Each year, I could create a new character. I remember in ninth grade I showed up in school in new wave drag—I borrowed one of my sister's sweaters, bra and my mom's Olivia Newton-John *Grease* shoes. And as I sashayed down the aisles, I got whistles and shocked stares. They thought I was the new girl on campus. I was just trying to emulate Olivia Newton-John. Drag or dress up allowed me entrance into an intoxicating world.

I recently talked to a friend of mine who when blocked as an actress was a very, very brilliant costume designer. When I met up with her years later, she was lurching toward acting, and I said to her, "Costume design gave you good experience into acting." And she seemed astonished I had made this observation. She seemed curious. "What do you mean by that?" she wanted to know. "Well, you know how to build a character from the ground up. When you were building costumes for people, you were gathering material for your own acting. You were creating in your mind all the characters you wanted to be."

I think she thought I was crazy. How could something so painful be helpful to what she really wanted to do? Well, serving her craft at one remove helped her to see how great she wanted to be. I knew I was on to something larger.

Making a character is all about the right costume. Ruth Gordon said, "A costume is part of a performance, if it's right, you keep afloat." The clothes you are wearing onstage always trigger an internal change. For me, I find that the shoes are important. The soles of the shoes help me dream of the soul I am creating. A costume can make or break a performance because it is what the audience actually sees. It plays into their psyches and affects them emotionally. When I approach a character, one of the first things I put together is the costume. This helps me to act. Creating a character is all about the right costume (bathing suit, gown, fingernails, etc.).

When I was creating the costume for my character Davis Davis in *Off Hollywood* (the script called for a "poor man's Orson Welles"), I drew a sketch in my notebook of him. I also used images from the storyboard the director had shown me. I rummaged through books of Orson Welles during the 1930s. I wore the vintage pants that I had auditioned with, a pair of 1940s suspenders I found at a thrift store, and a pair of brown 1930s wingtip shoes. The costume designer completed the costume with a large, white dress shirt, a funky "vintage" tie, and a tweed coat with a "What Would Orson Do?" button attached to it. Each element was discussed by the director, the costume designer, and myself. During the rehearsal process, I would rehearse in parts of the costume in order to keep "in character."

Finding the costume is fun. Don't only rely on the costume designer or wardrobe to build your character. Work with them. Help them in finding the right costumes for the character.

I enjoy going to thrift stores with all the characters hanging on the racks. I love to see a pair of pants, and my mind immediately can build a character. Often times, it's not literal, it's abstract . . . "That man really wore out his seams . . ." The mere act of putting a costume together can make a character come to life for us. Clothes can change your disposition. Clothes can change your mood. Clothes can change how you feel about the part you playing.

When I was creating the character of Cupid in *The Reindeer Monologues,* I designed my costume so he would be "gay" on sight. I wore brown platform shoes (like hooves), green silk pajama bottoms, and a red "disco" shirt. I topped it off with antlers spray-painted pink with Christmas ornaments sewn on to them. Every night, I got laughs on my entrance before I even opened my mouth.

This next task, I ask you to let go of your rational mind and jump in. Don't overthink this! First thought best thought.

Stop Dragging Your Feet

What is the good of drag? Drag is an ancient ritual. Drag is about personality and personae and the idea of playing around, goofing off, and singing along to the radio. Actors tend to get really cerebral and think their way into the character. This is an exercise that invites you to step into another person's shoes and have some fun in the process. It is good for moving out of the head and into the body.

Integrate what we have discussed in this chapter on costumes, entrances, and music. Use one from each element when you perform this three- to four-minute scene.

"I was resistant at first and I didn't want to come to class, but when I did it, I felt like I walked through the wall . . . All the barriers were torn down for me, and I really wanted to act . . ." a student exclaimed.

Try and be depressed when you're pretending you are somebody else. Just try it. See if it doesn't alter (lift) your mood and attitude.

This week, find a piece of music you like and perform a lip-synch. Dress up. Have fun with this. (No, you don't have to wear high heels and makeup, guys! But you can if you want!) The whole point of this exercise is to prove you don't have to have a lot of money to act. Use what you have.

Tasks

1. *Perform a scene from your "script reading."*

2. *Write an "I remember . . ." on how you made it.* Be sure to put in who helped you along, how you got to the top. You choose how you make it. Be specific and not literal. Pretend the whole universe is out to help you.

3. *Create a soundtrack for your character.*

4. *List all your artistic victories.* Spend time basking in your own limelight. Just list them. (e.g., I got the "Pink" video, I got my play produced, I got a rave review, etc.)

5. *Create a drag.* Find a piece of music you love and create a character around it. Bring this to class.

6. *My greatest moments.* Make a quick list of your greatest moments in your acting or life. (Yes, life is a stage, too.) You can go as far back as you want. These are the Oscar moments of your career or life. Some of mine: When I did *Legends,* I got applause on my exit almost every night. When I was in college, I did a mentally retarded character and I ate a cigarette and the audience loved it.

7. *How many "nos" have you heard lately?* Make a list of your current rejections. Wear them like badges of honor.

8. *Write a monologue from your "I remembers . . ."*

9. *Write in your notebook five different entrances for one character.* Do this throughout the rest of the course.

Week 6: Check-in

1. How many days did you do your "I remembers . . ."? Are they difficult for you? Are you writing them from a character's point of view yet?
2. What script did you read? This week make notes of different entrances made by different characters.
3. Are you remembering to put images in your notebook? Have you started to really splurge on your images? Have your pictures begun to change yet?
4. Have you noticed any synchronicity yet? What was it? (Did any acting opportunities come your way?)
5. Any other issues come up for you?

Week 7
Act 2, Scene 3

The universe will reward you for taking risks on it's behalf.
—Shakti Gawain

Acting Is "Action!"

Risk begins with willingness, saying "yes" to our dreams and ourselves. We take the courage to get our headshots together, to update the resume, to go on the audition, or to put a theater company together to showcase our work, yet we seldom see the miles we've traveled. If you do one thing a day, soon those little actions will trigger a change in the universe. Also as you expand and your career heats up, you can accomplish bigger and better things. It's always the first step that requires the most amount of faith. Sometimes, the hardest part of being a writer is opening the document and beginning typing. But once we take the small step, all fear falls away.

As blocked actors, we have a tendency to discount the small things we actually do. We forget the path we are on, the ground beneath us. We are constantly discounting and ignoring our positive steps forward. We are constantly living in the results and telling ourselves that it will never happen. "If only I did more!" the old story goes as we spin our wheels in the wrong line of questioning.

Grounding yourself in this one thing a day will increase your ability to take risk. I have found taking a small action when I don't "feel" like it, seems pointless, and even stupid. "Why are you doing this? No one cares!" My critic likes to scratch at my mind. I've learned to keep that old dinosaur trapped in the closet. Even when we seem to be stuck in the mud and not going forward, there are things moving for us. The universe doesn't stop dreaming just because we stop. The universe is on our side. God is for us. God wants us to succeed. We are the ones who stop and "think" about our acting dreams. Case in point:

I had a play *Attitudes and the Dance* produced! This was my big moment to shine, as actor and writer. I was proud of the work I spend months laboring over. Well, the play didn't unfold correctly. I had many problems I didn't know how to handle: I had unruly, lazy actors whose egos were bigger than their talent and a director afraid of confrontation. Needless to say, the production fell completely apart, got horrific reviews, and broke my desire to act. I thought I would never, ever get on stage again; I was mortally mortified, shocked, and hurt. If I had had my way (will), I would have withdrawn from the world to write and teach never to feel the heat of spotlights again! End of career.

But thank God, the world had other plans and ideas and dreams for me. My friend told me he was going to an audition, and before he went, I half-jokingly remarked, "If they need any drag queens, give them my number." And off he went only later to call me from the audition. "Stephen, you have to audition! This part is made for you! I'll drive you there."

And I remember wanting to waffle and say, "I don't know . . ." But I said "yes." I remember putting on makeup and showing up at the audition. I busted through the door and said in my Bette Davis voice, "Where's the director?!" I immediately began to work (own!) the room. I did a monologue from my show that bombed (this time all the humor and pathos were miraculously there). I read the sides, flirted with the producers, and I got the role. The new show *It Started with a Lie* was mounted on the exact same stage where I had "bombed," and I got some rave reviews and huge applause each night.

See, all the things that I had learned and practiced had sharpened me, and I had the one magic element: willingness. Willingness to show up when all the odds are stacked against you. Willingness is walking through the mysterious door to see where it will take you.

There is one weakness in people for which there is no remedy. It is the universal weakness of lack of ambition.
—Napoleon Hill

Be careful not to beat up on yourself if you find it challenging to make a move toward some goal. Dreams scare us, especially big dreams. I advocate taking one small action daily toward your dream. I think the big dream is the one your soul wants beyond all others. It is your job and responsibility to nurture and support yourself toward this dream. Save the drama for other people who don't have so much to lose. The big dream is the one you want the most, yet avoid the most. We avoid it because we were taught to be fearful of what would happen to us if we follow our acting dreams. At this point on the path, it's important to make lists of risks and follow through on them.

We are aiming at concentrating on small, doable actions we undertake and giving ourselves rewards and treats along the way. We don't need to beat ourselves up with harsh and critical judgments and endlessly lash out at our actor for our fears. Admit when you are afraid and the fear begins to soften. A slight turning over and seeing and writing out your accomplishments (both large and small!) can go a long way toward encouraging the little toddler actor. I remember, after my show was over, that I was being harsh and critical to everyone who stumbled across my path. That was nothing to the beating and slashing I was doing to myself. Nobody could do anything to help me. So what I needed to do was give myself some compassion. I had to love myself. Give yourself some credit. Some gold stars of your own for your accomplishment and willingness. We fail to recognize ourselves, our talents, and our dreams.

It takes great courage to show up and crawl up on to the stage. It's frightening. It's exciting, but it is not easy. For every risk you undertake, you should give yourself a nice treat. (I used to buy myself an ice cream cone if I went to commercial auditions because my inner actor hated them so much.)

Writing is done one word at a time. Acting is the same way. Acting is done with one small action built upon the other. Action by action is how acting takes place on screen or on stage. Just like life. Scene by scene it unfolds. Acting begins to have a life of its own. You must learn to evolve along with it. We begin to place one footstep in front of the other. We learn that acting is a process, in fact, a way of looking at life. We learn to build one character at a time. We learn to go by doing. Acting process is so confused with product. There is nothing wrong with "product," for I believe as an actor you are your own product and you always own it; however, your product is very malleable, constantly changing in flux, thus you are also constantly in process.

Acting is a series of committed choices. Commitment to a single action carried out moment by moment.

Finish the following sentence ten times.

I would love to act, but_____.

I would love to act, but I don't have an agent.
I would love to act, but I'm not in SAG.
I would love to act, but I'm broke.
I would love to act, but I'm working nine-to-five.
I would love to act, but everything is precast.
I would love to act, but my agent never sends me out.

Did you get a pretty volatile list of negatives? It's the "but" that keeps us behind. It's what we use to avoid taking risk. We can't take a risk and then immediately criticize and critique ourselves for taking it. The risk is the thing that counts in the end. I've used every one of the above excuses to keep me from acting. But I do know that each one is flimsy as a paper lantern and must be kicked under the carpet. What acting practice has begun to teach you is to act under all circumstances. Begin to practice your acting and the doors will start to swing open for you.

Building the House

I was recently discussing my method of acting and remarked, "All the homework I do on a part, the writing, the visualizing, the learning the lines, the costume, and voice is like building a giant house that I get to play in." Now, we are going to concentrate on "where" the action takes place in a scene. The environment is fun to explore in a scene. When you read a scene, make note of where the scene takes place and fill that room with as many specific details. The doors, the windows, and the furniture are all elements to utilize in your acting. How does your character feel about the space? Have they lived there for years (like the family in *You Can't Take It with You*)? Have they just moved in (like the characters in *Barefoot in the Park*)? Are you entering the room for the first time (like Blanche in *Streetcar Named Desire*)? Register these questions fully in your notebook.

When I was in rehearsals for *Come Back to the Five and Dime, Jimmy Dean, Dean,* my character was returning for a twenty-year reunion after leaving the town and having a sex change. I wrote in my journal, "This room is like entering a haunted house. All the memories of my past hang out like ghosts in each corner of the room. The room is dusty with age like looking through an antique mirror. My youth is in every corner. My boyhood, my uprooting, and my demise are waiting for me when I enter through that dust-covered screen door. Each table, each chair where we carried on our sacred meetings of the James Dean fan club holds a memory as real as the salt-and-pepper shakers."

I did this writing before I even set foot on the stage. I imagined what the room would look, sound, and taste like while I was in the script reading stages of the play. I wanted to connect my character's sense of isolation, dread, and hope to the physical objects of the room. I wrote long lists on what I thought the room would have in it from the clues I was given in the script.

In our acting scenes, we must imagine a lot of things while in rehearsal because you don't actually use the furniture or room until late in the rehearsal process (the week of "tech" in theater and the day of shooting in a film). When I first make contact with the physical, working set, I will walk around it for hours to get it in my body. I will touch the doorknobs, the windows, the drapes, the tables, the chairs, the water cooler, the desk, the drawers, the stove, and the oven to endow them with my own energy.

The stage where you act is very important. Furniture on stage is not usual. It can be used to bring out character elements. The piano Mozart plays on, the bed Blanche sleeps on, the wheelchair Joan Crawford sits in *Baby Jane,* the moldy bookshelves in *Who's Afraid of Virginia Woolf,* and the staircases that Bette Davis stomps down in all her movies. Each character has a relationship to those rooms.

This week, in your scenes, I want you to take notice of your character's physical surrounding. Examine everything in the room that is given in the script and endow it with your own memories of it.

"Properties" of Acting

After we look at the big picture of the environment, we go down to the props. Props are also another element of acting that can be utilized to help bring the character to life. The props (phone, TV, computer, martini glass, candle, pictures, pens, paper, dishes, beach ball, blankets, etc.) must be endowed with the character's relationship with them in a specific way to arouse feelings.

When I was prepping for the movie *Off Hollywood,* I worked with the set designer to help make the space my own. Davis lives in a storage unit in Hollywood. Davis is a writer-director, so I brought in my journals, my pens and markers, and drew pictures of the character's storyboards and hung them on the wall. I brought in my great-grandmother's blanket that she crocheted, and even my pet monkey that I carried around as a child (I didn't think Davis would have a teddy bear). I wanted *each* thing in the room to connect to me in a very honest way.

How does the character interact with these items in the scene? How do they pour tea? How do they hold a cigarette? How do they talk on the phone?

Make lists in your acting notebook this week of the props you can use. When I am in rehearsals, I often will bring in "substitute" props to play with. When I was rehearsing for *Off Hollywood,* I brought in a satchel, a beat-up script, and an overcoat when I was prepping the opening scene where Davis gets kicked out of the movie studio for the thousandth time. I found that the props grounded me in the physical of the scene and gave my character something to concentrate on while he delivered his "epic" speeches about how "Hollywood is doomed!" I could not have played the scene with truth without these objects in place.

The props in a scene can help you build your character. In the case of Davis, his script was his baby, his brainchild, and each time I handled it, I treated it with kid gloves. It helped me breathe life into my role.

When I watch Shirley Maclaine, I'm always mindful of how she uses props. In the scene in *Postcards from the Edge,* when she's having an argument with her daughter in the kitchen, watch how she makes her shake in the blender. I always exclaim, "She's a real prop actress!" because she uses every prop to say something specific about the character. Another good actress to watch is Sally Field in *Steel Magnolias* as she cracks eggs into a bowl while making a cake while she's fighting with her daughter. Both these woman are known for their riveting, emotional performances.

This week look at each prop in your scene and write a little story about them. How did the character get them? What does the character feel about them? During the remaining scene work, bring in props and work with them in class. Also while you are going through your day, think of the things you handle as props in a play and think of ways you can say your lines while handling these various objects.

Scene from "I Remembers..."

In light of what we've been working on, let's put it to use. This week, I want you to write a tiny scene from your "I remembers . . ." (No, it doesn't have to be Shakespeare or perfect.) I want you to keep in mind the set and the props when you write it. Below is another scene from *Pyramid Scheme* in which the main character gets fired. (Notice how I've used the cubicle, the desk, the computer, the envelope, and the mail tub.)

(Dick stands at his cubicle with his supervisor, Edwin. Edwin pushes a white envelope across the desk to Dick.)

Edwin: I hate to do this, but we need to downsize . . .
Dick: What?
Edwin: We have to cut corners . . .
Dick: Well, who is going to answer the phone?
Edwin: Sandra in production . . .
Dick: Hunter's Sandra . . .
Edwin: They are liquidating that department . . .
Dick: I'm being fired so Hunter's girlfriend can have a job?
Edwin: She has kids . . .
Dick: Great. *Great!*
Edwin: I just want you to know, you've been a wonderful employee. We hate to lose you! I really fought for you! If you need a letter of recommendation or anything, don't hesitate to ask.
Dick: How about a loan . . .
Edwin: What?
Dick: Nothing . . . Do you want me to finish out the day?
Edwin: You can leave now. Just give me your key before you leave.

(Edwin walks away. Dick, in a rage, turns off his computer and begins to pack his belongings from his desk into a mail tub.)

Tasks

1. *Perform your "I remember..." monologue.*

2. *Dress up like a movie star.* Really dress up to the nines. And go out and turn some heads. Remember to write about it.

3. *List all your artistic wounds.* Don't stop to examine why or question them. Just list them. (e.g., I dyed my hair canary yellow and "they" still didn't cast me, I didn't even get a callback, etc.)

4. *Write a scene from your "I remembers..."*

5. *Examine the environment in your scene.*

6. *History of props.* Write out a full inventory of the props to use in your scenes. Bring props to class you use in your scenes.

Week 7: Check-in

1. How many days did you do your "I remembers..."? Are you more comfortable telling more of your story?
2. What script did you read? Did you take notice of the physical environment and also take notes about props used? What themes did you find "hot"?
3. Are you remembering to put images in your notebook? Now begin to add actual photos of yourself "living" the acting dream. (reviews you'd like, awards you want to win, roles you'd like to play...) Seeing is believing.
4. Have you noticed any synchronicity yet? What was it? (Did any acting opportunities come your way?)
5. Any other issues come up for you? Have you been tempted to stop acting?

Week 8
Act 2, Scene 4

*Don't guess. Don't be half-hearted. Say yes and mean it.
That's why so many half-hearted auditions happen;
because you don't commit yourself.*
—Michael Shurtleff

Save the Drama for the Stage!

Keep in mind everyone you work with remembers what you do. It will come around again. Save the drama for the role. Don't be a diva unless you have the talent to back it up. And if you are really talented, you don't need the "backstage" drama. You know the value of your work, and you simply do your job. It is insecurity on some level that make actors "act up" during the rehearsal process. I always say, "UNLESS YOU HAVE A TALENT AS HUGE AS JUDY GARLAND'S THEN YOU HAVE NO RIGHT TO PULL A DIVA! SHUT UP, LEARN YOUR LINES, AND HIT YOUR MARK!" I've worked with very green (young) actors who had more "enthusiasm" than talent. Why do I mention this? Because you will be remembered as either (a) hardworking, inspiring, and uplifting or (b) difficult, demanding, and not very talented. Make sure if you are being dramatic, it's for the good of the show. Make sure it's for "how can I make this piece better?" not "how can I make myself look good or better than everyone else?" As actors, we have a choice to work in harmony or be a complete nightmare.

Directing the play on the sidelines is *not* the actor's job. I've seen many actors attempt to do this. This is a controlling device and a feeble attempt to avoid their own acting responsibilities. It's an evasive trick, and it never works. It's a way to hide our own insecurities. We all want to do good work on the stage, but raging against another actor will never get you to where you want to go. The only job of the actor is to play a character and all the rest is talk.

The phrase that I can't tolerate to hear actors say is: "I need *you* to give me _____ in order for me to do my part!" Actors who demand other actors give them something (an emotion, a look, or a response) in order to do their job are misplacing their energies and manipulating the other actor. This is not playing by the rules of acting. The director is the *only* person who should ever tell an actor what to do. Don't demand anything from anyone except yourself. And don't tolerate other obnoxious "attitude problems" from other actors. Focus on your *own* process. I was recently working on a movie and the other actor skipped a line, and I "acted as if" he had said the line and kept acting, not missing a beat. The director was happy I didn't stop because I kept the shot! I could have stopped and snapped, "You didn't say *your line*!" to the other actor, but why add chaos? Now, sometimes you are going to have to put your foot down!

A few years ago, I was working with a highly dramatic, egomaniac (in the play *The Matchmaker*) who had worked on *Baywatch* (big, fat deal, right?!) He thought he was God's gift to the acting craft. I was playing Barnaby and he was playing Cornelius, and we were supposed to be best friends. I tried to give him looks and glances the first month of rehearsals because I wanted to bond with him and create chemistry between the characters. But this actor didn't have his act together (wouldn't learn his lines, debated with the director, and directed every actor in the production) and ignored all the good "stuff" I was giving him. As the rehearsal progressed, he slowly turned each cast member against each other and then against the director. He created such a dramatic display until the show was a terrible ordeal with the cast divided down the middle and the director threatening to walk out. At one point, right near opening night, he turned to me red in the face fury flaming ready to flip his blonde toupee and said, "Stephen, you need to give me_____!" And I turned to him and said, "No! *You* need to do your own work. My character is already set." And I watched him explode to the director how "difficult" I was. It was the first time I stood up for myself, my work, and my talent, and it felt great. I don't model my acting for someone else's convenience in order for them to look good. Most especially if they are *not* prepared. I say this as a warning to you young actors who might butthead with someone who feels competitive and manipulative to you because they have "more experience." I repeat, "The director is the *only* person who should ever tell an actor what to do."

To make a long story short, guess who got the laughs opening night? Who has continued to work? Me. Despite this over-the-top diva's view of my acting. He didn't have a positive attitude. He didn't want to serve the play only but his big ego. This type of behavior can dampen the morale of an entire show. It's true what they say, "One bad apple can destroy the whole batch." Remember when you are acting, you are demonstrating who you are.

It took me years to trust my talents and to not give in when I know I'm right. Protecting ourselves and having the courage to take a stand is a learned skill. Acting practice teaches us how to do these things with much more ease and grace. The words "I don't think that's the best idea" or "I think that might work" will form on our lips as we keep gaining strength as actors.

As actors, we have a tendency to want to stop the rehearsal process and "think" about what we are doing. We chat with other actors about the character, the subtext, and the motivations when we are actually stalling for time and weaseling out of our work. I'm just being honest. Acting is best done on its feet and moving not sitting discussing the beats; this can waste huge amounts of time. Instead of finding the beats or nuances in the scene as we run it, we have a habit of wanting to discuss the scene too much instead of running it. Discussing the scene too much with the other actor can be dangerous.

It takes us out of the realm of make-believe and fantasy or let's pretend. Acting is not literal, acting is messy and inspired. We avoid doing our acting, because we are fearful of what will happen if we simply choose anything (even the wrong thing) and stick to it 100 percent. Let the character reveal itself to us as we go. Instead of trusting ourselves and our acting, we avoid the risk and excitement by throwing the "thinking" water on our scenes. We freeze up. The ideas no longer flow. Creation goes zipping out the window. Now I'm not saying that we should never discuss and search for our characters, but I've learned the hard way that acting is best done when we don't overthink it. And a lot of that homework must be done in private, *not* the rehearsal space when the clock is ticking. Now there will be times when you are trying to play a specific moment and it's not coming and you will have to analyze why with the director. I was recently working on a movie and couldn't get a line the way the director had it in mind, and he pulled me aside and we discussed it. I told him what I thought the character was doing in that moment, and the director explained that he might want something else and suggested I play it that way, and it worked. This was a very quick five-minute discussion.

Now, there is a way to approach other actors. You ask for their help. You seek out the part of them that is trying to act with you. I worked with two wonderful actresses in a piece I wrote called *Legends and Bridge*. When we began the work, I thought they were too accomplished for me. But now I see why they were right for me. We all contributed to each other. We suggested things, but did not demand them. The actor's skin has to be both tough and vulnerable. We have to be influenced by things, but strong enough to say no when something doesn't work for us. What I loved about working with these two actresses is their professionalism. We all showed up and did the work. We each contributed our greatness and our gifts, not our ego's demand for the highest position. When you work in harmony and trust on stage or TV or film, it shows. I don't think audiences are dumb. They know when people are getting along. They can feel the chemistry or lack of.

I once talked with a gifted but "blocked" actor who told me a story that I find a lot of actors do. He told me he was being signed by a *big* agency, and simultaneously, he had a small manager interested in his work. He told me that the manager had a small client base and was very interested in his work, but the actor had to prepare three monologues. The actor in turn said, "I'm offended that you're having *me* audition for you. Just sign me." And he refused to do the *work* of finding three monologues and trying out for this manager who could benefit him. Two crosscurrents were at odds here: First, the actor, being as studied and cultured as he was, should already have monologues in his back pocket. Second, the actor was unwilling to take the risk of auditioning. We all have to audition. That's the fact. He wanted it the easy way. "Just sign me, because I'm too proud to submit to an audition." Is not humility and trusting your acting, it's saying, "I'm too talented and experienced to do the work!" This is stubborn, hardheaded, and ego-based thinking. No, it does not work that way. Do the work and prove to the manager or director your willingness to work. This is the kind of actor who only wants to work for the paycheck. Actors act. They act for fun, they act at readings, and they act, period. I can't state it any clearer or cleaner. If you want to act, you must have the willingness to do the tools of your craft.

When I was being considered for the role of Davis in *Off Hollywood,* I spent two months auditioning for the role. Two long months of learning lines and working with my costar in what was termed "Davis Camp" where they were testing not only my "talent" but my character as well, and I passed with flying colors. I memorized the scenes. I worked with them day and night, and at the end, I was *rewarded* with a wonderful lead in a film. Friends around me at the time thought I was nuts to go out on a limb like this for "a part" and thought it was unorthodox and unprofessional, but I knew the part was a once-in-a-lifetime role that was tailor-made for me.

I see that, in this essay, I have talked a lot about the kinds of "backstage" drama that can ensue when you act. I wish I could tell you younger actors that it's always a cakewalk and everyone gets along like a happy family. I have seen it be more like a dysfunctional family more often than not. People will have different ways of working—people will be dominating, rude, and mean sometimes. Remember that we're dealing with acting that is sensitive and psychic in nature. I'm very vulnerable when I act because I open a lot of channels to do my work. I *need* access to all my emotions from joy down to depression so I can draw on them when I perform. The "backstage" stuff can distract and close the channel down.

When I read that a "star" is standoffish on the set and doesn't like to be hounded by people, I thought they were being rude, but they are trying to *concentrate*. When I was doing *Off Hollywood,* I had to shut out everything on the set in order to play the part. And anytime you do a show, there are going to be "dramas" that you can't avoid.

Relationships on the set or in the rehearsal must be built on respect and boundaries. I find that often because we want so much to perform and it's such a challenge even to get cast, that we often have poor boundaries when we are in the middle of creativity, but we must have those walls in place; otherwise, chaos will ensue. Just be careful when you're cocreating with others either in class or in the professional world. I once was doing a workshop with a fellow and we rehearsed the scene in the hallway, and when I rehearse cold copy, I like to get the general feel of it with the other actor, and turn on my "secret" magic tricks when I'm before the casting director or audition.

I worked on the copy with this actor and said, "I think I'm ready!" And he said, "Stephen, that sucked," and my head spun around like the girl in *The Exorcist*, and I sharply said, "You know, it's not your job to tell me how to act. I'll read the copy one more time with you and we'll go in and do it for the casting director." And I read it one more time with a bit more pizzazz and then went into the room and killed! See, I've learned no to shoot my entire cannon at rehearsal.

Just like before, I do a stand-up comedy gig. I don't stand backstage yukking it up and talking to other comedians before I go on! I stay very close to myself and don't even run my set. To me it's like taking a history test in school. You either know it or you don't! I look at performing like a magic show. I don't like to show people my tricks! A character I worked on was obsessed with Orson Welles who was a magician as well as a giant filmmaker. Those who watch me seem to think it's "easy" to do what I do. Part of an actor's job is to synthesize everything, and once you take the stage, you let it fly!

I know comedians who'll go out and "wing it" and some are *great* at it! I'm not! I'm very shy and introverted by nature and get fumbled up when I don't clearly know what I'm going to say up there! I do my best when I know exactly what I'm doing, and on that solid foundation, I can attack the audience.

I was doing a show with a woman, and for weeks, we were supposed to hook up and prepare a "bit", but something always came up: she got the flu, her car broke down, her son got stabbed . . . and pretty soon, the day arrived and I said, "Okay we haven't rehearsed . . . shall we cancel?" And she said, "Oh, I'll get there a few hours early and we'll go over it and rehearse." Well, the night rolled around and I showed up at 6:00 p.m. (dressed as Bette Davis, no doubt!), and she dragged in at seven and needed to "get ready," and so our rehearsal was literally "just say something," and we had no clear banter and we *bombed!* Lesson learned: *Don't go up unprepared!*

Auditions Are Not Crisis!

Why do we actors have to stop for two weeks when we get an audition? We have the build up and the talks about how *big* and important the audition and blah, blah, blah . . . Talk, talk! "Talk is cheap," the old saying goes. Actions are what we need. When I'm auditioning, I'll rehearse it as much as I possibly can and then I send friends e-mails (prayers needed!) and then I show up.

We think we need to discuss the part . . . "I'm going to be famous," and other nonsense. We get on the phone and start blabbing and we lose great creative moments, and what we should be doing is preparing and taking actions, not talking. Some actors then spend time wallowing in the self-flagellation after the audition: "Oh, I did it wrong! I was terrible!" or "I was great and they didn't notice! They are so dumb! I know they're going to cast me! I woulda, coulda, shoulda . . ." No, don't go there with yourself. Once I leave the audition room, I consider it *done!* If I get called back, *great!* If I don't, I go on to the next audition. My motto with auditions is "*next!*"

Please, take it from someone who used to beat himself up after all auditions, "Oh, I did it all wrong. You did it so *bad* . . . You're no good!" Please be gentle with yourself and move beyond it. I knew an actress who would call me for two weeks after each audition and bark at me how bad it was and why she didn't get cast. She would analyze the entire event over and over endlessly. And I wanted to say, "Why aren't you putting more out?" Now, if you really, truly, and honestly gave a crappy audition, you might ask *yourself* some questions: Was I totally present? Did I prepare? Did anything before (or during) the audition toss me? (the conversation in the waiting room, traffic, the "bad" copy, and no place to park?) Why did I freeze up?

I once went on an audition for an improv group, and I felt very eager and excited before I got there. I wore some funny character clothes and felt "up," but as I waited in the lobby, I started to sense something was "off." There was only one other guy there to audition and the guy running the audition had only one other person there to do improv with us. Well, I thrust myself into it and tried to stay in the moment and create funny characters and say funny things (things that I'm pretty *great* at doing under better circumstances!), but I found myself feeling really *out* of sorts, and my inner critic started to raise up and not give me anything good! And I started to feel really, really angry at the entire situation and shutting down until I just closed down completely in one scene and knew I had completely bombed that audition!

Needless to say, they never called me, and I felt like the worst actor in the world! What I did not do is talk to a million people about it! I said, "Well, better luck next time! I hope they find what they are looking for, and I'm sure I'll find out what I need!" And the next audition I went on was for a burlesque troupe and I got it! I let it rip at the audition and walked away feeling really good! So never make one audition life or death or give it too much build up! Now that being said some roles and some things you prepare for you are going to *really, really* want and work your butt off and guess what? The role will go to someone else. Or the director will cast her boyfriend. We can't control these factors! But we can condition ourselves like strong racehorses to not get sidetracked when we're thrown off the track.

Don't get strung out on one part! Someone once told me there are two kinds of parts, the ones that are yours and the ones that are not! This can really toss us over-emotional (sensitive) actors who believe we should get every part that's *ours!* I once had a student who would put herself through the ringer before, during, and after *every* audition! She'd replay the entire audition scene out over and over again, and unfortunately, they were not always the positive ones that she'd "replay." I said to her, "You might want to zip the lip and not tell those stories so much . . ." But she wanted to agonize about the parts that she *should* have gotten!

This is a very tempting stance and damaging as well! It's all right to "mourn" the roles you don't get, but not too long. Madonna says she mourns for twenty-four hours when something she doesn't like happens. I *love* that advice because she's learned to keep moving, and she's a multimillionaire. I once went out for a part in a play about Oscar Wilde playing Lord Alfred Douglas (Wilde's lover). I prepared for the role by reading all I could about their tortured relationship, and I dyed my hair blonde and went and read for the role and did *great!* Well, the director loved me, the producer thought I was "too short," and I remember clearly the day I got the call from the director that I didn't get cast, and for the first time in my career I cried! I took my notebook, walked to my favorite restaurant, and as the sun went down, tears streamed down my face! I mourned the loss of not getting cast, and I sat and wrote about it, but the next day I was back to auditioning again. I didn't bury the pain anymore. Instead, I said to my actor, "I know this hurts . . . especially the 'too short' part, but I'll give you a treat, a reward, and we'll still act." That was a major revelation for me. Knowing I could survive the rigors of preparing for a part, auditioning, and then getting let down.

I was deeply disappointed in college when I wasn't cast as Bomber in *Picnic,* and then ten years later, I got cast in the same role! My agent sent me to an audition for the transsexual role in *Come Back to the Five and Dime, Jimmy Dean, Jimmy Dean,* and I dressed in "drag," went to the director's house (driving my not air-conditioned VW cabriolet), and his assistant thought I was one of the women auditioning for the "women" parts in the play, she was shocked that I was a man. I had memorized the big monologue in act 2 and started to do it for the director, but halfway through, the telephone rang and he answered it. (The nerve!) I just kept going while he talked on the phone and watched me. Try to live *that* down. I didn't book that one. Two years later, I went in "dressed up" again at the Hermosa Beach Playhouse and played that part and got wonderful reviews and a triumph personally. So don't hang on to those auditions. Go to them, do the best you can, and then leave it behind. If you're really meant to play a part, it will one day be yours. I'm still longing to play Mozart in *Amadeus.* (I wasn't cast in high school).

I once spent months preparing to audition for Del Shore's play *Cheatin'* in a role that was played by Leslie Jordan, but the season of plays got canceled and I didn't even get to audition! But just getting ready was fun!

We get hooked into the drama. We lure ourselves in by making every audition such a "big deal" that we forget all about our lives. "*Oh, this is going to make me!*" and we are off in another world. Instead of focusing on the work, we let it toss us away. Another poisonous thing we do is tell a million people how big and important this role is to us, how right we are; we don't take the time to center ourselves, and we have so much drama to it that we show up ill-prepared or taxed out. The cure is respect for your actor. Keep quiet about it. Don't build it up to such a big deal. Don't send yourself up the river. And then we don't get the part we spent two *more* weeks in the drama of why we didn't get the part and bemoan and berate ourselves. As the great director Tyrone Guthrie used to say, "*On!*" That means reboot yourself and get back to the auditions. Sitting and crying doesn't help. While you're doing that, the other actors in the world are being cast. I'm not saying ignore your feelings and disappointments. I'm saying don't wallow in them. This too shall pass. And believe me, it will pass so much quicker and quieter if you move beyond it!

Quick Fix

Okay, so you're miserable. You can't move. You think this whole acting thing is just a bug that you should shake. You've got the blues of creativity. You wonder at why you started in the first place. You are telling yourself that you can't go another mile. You feel like you should burn all those headshots and do something real. The day job and selling Avon are looking better than acting. Okay. We all get there! We all go through the rough patch of self-doubt. Okay this is the quick fix: Pick up a script. Do it. And Open it randomly and begin to read out loud. Do it. *Now*.

If you did it, how did it feel? Did you find yourself getting a little into it? Excited? Were you scared? Often we get tossed off the game board by fear. Did you hear that old doubt start chatting you up? "You're no good?" Or did it liberate you? Did it feel stupid? Good! Whatever it brought up for you is a good thing! I suggest you use this tool often. It's good medicine for those blues that strike. It's also a great way to get a cold reading in place.

We are rarely kind to ourselves when we are acting. We are taught and trained we must do it perfectly—that's our ego. We believe we must beat up and punish ourselves when we are attempting to learn acting. We forget gentleness and small, steady stream of actions. We set our goals way too high and beat ourselves up mercilessly when we fail to meet them. Expect and demand too much, too soon, too quickly, and expect to get discouraged. I think attitude is most important along with gentleness and kindness. Remember this and go slow (which our egos hate). You are healing, and heath takes time to stabilize and form. That's why acting practice is essentially doing one small thing and building up to the larger things. But for now, only stay rooted in the process and try to avoid the perfection.

I Booked It!

"You got the part!" What wonderful words! What scary words, too! Because now you get to do the work (play)! You get to now put everything that we've been doing in "acting practice" together. You will find that you will be excited and afraid. This is good! You will get to learn new lessons. Remember all strong muscles you have built in your "acting practice" and put them to use. You can use your "I remembers . . ." when you approach the character, the scenes, and even situations backstage.

You can use your acting notebook to keep you grounded and safe. You can use your script reading skills to find clues in the script to play.

In just eight short weeks, you have come a long way to healing your actor. There have been stumbles, there have been laughs and even tears, but you have walked through them. Be very proud of yourself right now. Give yourself a break and a treat. We never do the acting thing perfectly, but we are now in the rapids of it, and even on the worst days we know we're on the road to healing. Next week, we will start to work on "the business" side of acting.

You might do a quick list of things you've "booked" in the past to spur yourself on. (Here is my list!)

Some Roles I've Booked

The first role I ever booked after "unblocking" as an actor was a community theater production of *Picnic*. The director later told me that I got the role because of my size and because of my voice. (The parts of me I always want to change!)

I booked the Colorado Lotto commercial, and the director said that he cast me because, at the audition, I did a double take at the six feet guy who I was reading with. The director said he fell off his chair!

I booked a Nevada Water commercial where I danced around in my blue Speedo! (Talk about talent in the raw!) I went to the audition in my Speedo and a pair of little kid goggles I bought at the drugstore on my way to the audition. I wore a pair of knee-length shorts hoping they were kidding about the Speedo, but nope, they asked me to take them off! I was not in the best shape and I certainly am no supermodel, but I *did it!* And I booked it. They flew me out to Vegas, and I got paid handsomely! I *risked*.

I once hitchhiked all the way to Malibu for a callback and booked a Hewlett Packard commercial because I was short.

I was cast as the transsexual Joanne in *Come Back to the Five and Dime, Jimmy Dean, Jimmy Dean* after I dressed up in drag, learned the monologue, and "fooled" everyone at the audition (many who knew me before) and the director! She later said, "It was the most prepared audition I've ever seen!"

The director of the movie *Off Hollywood* told me that as soon as I poked my head in the doorway and he saw me, *he knew!* I wore my old 1930s vintage coat and a pair of tweed pants and carried a prop (a nine-hundred-page screenplay!). The script read, "A poor man's Orson Welles." So I dressed up like the part!

Tasks

1. *Reruns: My life on prime time!* List ten positive things that have happened to you in your acting!

    1. When the director called me and said I got the part.
    2. When I booked the part in *Jimmy Dean*.
    3. When I killed at the Comedy Store.
    4. When my agent called and said I booked the national commercial.
    5. When I got the residual check for the national commercial.
    6. When the show I was in got rave reviews.

    Now that you have a good little list, pick one and rerun it in your mind for a full thirty seconds until you feel good!

2. *I booked it:* List ten roles that you've booked (*or ten jobs you've landed*).

3. *Buried treasure:* List ten dreams or projects that you've given up on! Now ask why? Who hurt your feelings? Did you show your comedy to someone who shot it down or said "that's not funny," or did you get horrible reviews in a good movie? We are looking for the enemy here! If it was someone who was problematic or noncommunicative, write them down. Do you see any patterns? Have you let someone slide?

    I once made a quick list of folks who could be considered for my "mastermind" also known as the "inner circle." It amazed me when

I did this spot-check inventory how many people got ruled off by just having a bad attitude or "no ambition" or lack of enthusiasm. I was once working with a guy who was a cowriter on a project, and each time I got a piece of good news about it: a new door opening, a lead of some kind, his response was, "We'll see" instead of "*Thank you!* You've really worked hard on my behalf!" I was once working with a manager who was supposed to be sending out our script ("pitching" we call it in Hollywood!), and she always had an excuse: "The moon is full, they don't take calls on Fridays . . . I'm waiting to hear back from so-and-so's office", and after many scripts like this, I said, "At this rate she'll sell our wares in about seventy years!" I had another agent who I worked for, and I actually made pitch calls to production companies, got the script into over fifty hands, and when it came time for her to follow up, she had a bizillion excuses for not pitching. My favorite was: "My son stole my car and is missing!" And then after that drama settled down, she had another something to keep her from calling those companies!

So write down those people and situations on a list and then share it with a trusted friend. This helps soften the pain! Take them to coffee and let yourself admit you were banged up!

4. *Create a new you from the old you*. Instead of throwing out those old headshots and resumes, use them to do the "placemat process." On the left side, write what you intend to do that day and on the right-hand side write what you want the universe to do! (This is very fun creative way of cocreating with the universe.)

5. *List ten roles that you want to play*. They can be characters or specific roles from your script reading.

    1. Star
    2. Boss
    3. Director
    4. Hollywood writer
    5. "Hollywood" guy

6. *Perform your "I remember . . ." scene.*

Week 8: Check-in

1. How many days did you do your "I remembers . . ."? Are they difficult for you? Are you writing them from a character's point of view yet?
2. What script did you read? Remember that reading a play gives us a ground and fills the form. Have you found a specific type of role that you're repeatedly drawn to? Have you paid attention to themes that you like best?
3. Are you remembering to put images in your notebook? By putting images in, we are visualizing our lives. Seeing is believing.
4. Have you noticed any synchronicity yet? What was it? (Did any acting opportunities come your way?)
5. Any other issues come up for you? Have you been tempted to stop acting?

Week 9
Act 3, Scene 1

Where Is My Career?

Now that you've made it this far on your acting trail, we are going to look at the dragon called "marketing" yourself. This throws a lot of actors. "I just want to act!" I would say, but I didn't know in exactly what capacity. I acted in theater for many years before I realized I wanted to do TV and film work. Theater had given me great training as an actor, but I wish I had been more clear when I started. I was the "just give me *anything"* kind actor until I got cast as the lead in *Off Hollywood,* and my entire geography as an actor changed. I knew I was funny on theater and stand-up comedy (I even played the Comedy Store), but on film, I became extraordinary. There is something about the screen that loves my size and voice.

So let's ask: Where are you? Where is your career?

Now this is like putting a town on a map. Let's say you're in Dallas, Texas, but you want to be in New York City, well, you're going to have to move yourself there by foot, taxi, car, airplane, or bus. And you're going to have to go northeast. That is a different journey than going from Dallas to Los Angeles.

When you can identify where *exactly* you *are,* you can start to figure out where you want to go and how you can get there. There are many, many methods to get there.

Now ask: Where do I *want* to go?

Have you been doing mostly theater but long to do TV/film work? Have you been doing "bit" parts in small budget movies and want to move to the next level? Have you not performed in ten years and want to move back on to the stage or camera?

You'll need a little "action" plan, with step-by-step instructions, and you'll need to tell someone your plan so they can help you to see it and to help chart your progress with you. This is where the "acting buddy" will come into play. You can find this acting buddy in an acting workshop, in your circle of friends, or even online in a pinch.

Have some compassion for yourself if you are in a small town and not living in Hollywood. Acting can be done anywhere. I've been in Hollywood for many years and have seen as many "blocked" actors as I've seen in my hometown Bedford, Texas. Right now, we are just trying to establish where we are and finding ways to move toward it, even with small steps.

It's always a good idea at this point in the process to ask: What kind of acting do I want to do? Do I want to act on Broadway? (If the answer is yes, do stage work and point yourself to NYC.) Do I want to act in movies? (If the answer is yes, start making little movies and point your car toward Hollywood.) Do I want to act on sitcoms? Do I want to do stand-up comedy? Do I want to act in plays that I write? Do I want to do commercials? Do I want to be a late-night talk show host? Do I want to be in musicals?

You might find yourself wanting to do several of those, but one or two will be your "hottest" ones. Go back to week 1 and look at your "Vein of Gold" list. What themes do you resonate most with? Comedy, drama, biography, sitcom, or commercial? Look back at your "script reading." What types of scripts really hooked your interest?

In your scene work in class, what did you feel you were *best* at?

Go through your notes and write out on paper the types of scripts you like and the characters you thought were best suited to you.

In your acting career, don't be uprooted or discouraged by periods of dormancy. God is refreshing you and preparing you for bigger things. But don't be lazy and not practice. Practice. Practice. Practice. Practice until it comes around again.

We act because we must act. Every time we act, we are showing courage, bravery, and passion. Use these affirmations to bolster your courage this week.

Acting Affirmations:

My acting is God's will for me.
My acting leads to good.
I have a divine right to act.
Acting is my natural state.
I love myself and my acting.
Acting is my job.
My acting leads to success.
I am *now* a successful actor.

Taking aim: How do you view your career? How do you want to approach it? Which direction can you shoot your arrow? There are a million different ways to act. All of them help you. Be open to them all. Avoid the "I can do it all alone!" syndrome. Ask for help. Surround yourself with people who encourage your dreams. Avoid people who try to tell you practical advice. Don't listen! Listen and follow your heart.

Attention! Target Shoppers! Creating Your Package

As actors, we have a tendency to take things for granted. We are often blind to what we do better than anyone else. Through using the tools in this workbook, we have started to arouse those questions. We have started to see ourselves in a new light. As actors, we have to awaken to these gifts and put them to use. Everything about *you* can be fuel for your acting. It's a matter of paying attention to every detail.

Avoid the thinking monster. Don't "I don't know" yourself to death. Act as if you do know and stick to a choice all the way to the end. You'll learn and grow if you do. Don't hesitate at this point in your acting even though you don't know all the answers ahead of time.

This is a very important step in your self-definition as an actor! Who *are you?* How do you view yourself and your talent? These are very important questions we're going to explore.

If you've been following the clues closely and doing acting practice, you've learned a *lot* about yourself as an actor. Now we're going to tackle something very important: *packaging yourself.* When I first started to act, I had no concept of who I was or how I wanted to be viewed by the world, it was very general, "I'm just an actor . . . ," but it was when I got specific that I started to gain insight and power.

It took seven years of encouragement from my partner Chuck to *stop* hiding behind "drag" and admit that I was "funny" as a man! He kept saying to me "You're a comedic genius," and it took many years of struggle for me to admit that I was a real actor and not a cheap impersonator. (Although, by doing all those "drag" characters, I became a powerful actor and created some sensational roles for myself.)

When I first started to act as a guy, I remember I felt like a real lump of coal in a diamond mine. The best image I could come up with was: "If Woody Allen and Bette Midler had a baby, it would be C. Stephen Foster!" But I applied the acting practice to myself, and I discovered something very vital: *Chuck was right! I was funny!* What others had to really work hard at came like breathing to me! No wonder I felt like an oddball! I was one! The only person I could think of who reminded me of myself was actor Leslie Jordan (the short guy on the sitcom *Will & Grace*). What a model!

So that's how I started to "package" myself: "The younger Leslie Jordan." I could use all those qualities that I thought were faults to my advantage: funny, short, high-voice, and off-center! My agent found it easier to "pitch" me with that image in mind! I found it easier to spot roles that were great for me!

When I first started going to casting director workshops, they would say, "You remind me of that short guy on *Will & Grace* (Leslie Jordan)," and I would find it the best compliment in the world. I had finally found my "market."

One of the best experiences I had was when I played Cupid in *The Reindeer Monologues*. I could have sworn I channeled Leslie when I played that part! I came out in a flurry to ABBA's "Dancing Queen," which later became how I opened my stand-up routine. I've always liked the quirky, offbeat kind of roles: Michael in *Creeps*, Peter in *Romeo and Juliet*, Cupid in *Reindeer Monologues*, and Mozart in *Amadeus*.

Now, how would you "package" yourself? Comedic, leading man/woman, dramatic, soap opera, musical, abstract, sexy female, or father or mother? Remember, a quick way to see how you package yourself is to look at the scripts you've read and made a note of the characters you're attracted to, and this will give you insight into yourself. Try to unearth the qualities that make you "stand out" from the crowd. What parts of you are unique and different?

Answer the following:

1) What parts of my physical appearance are different?
2) Do I have an unusual voice or accent?
3) What "stars" do I resemble?
4) What roles have I already been cast in?

Remember, as an actor you *are* selling something. You are peddling *you!* You are packaging and marketing yourself and your gifts to agents, to directors, to casting directors, and to the world.

"Attention: Casting! *You!*"

Another way to find out our market is to explore roles you've *already* played both in your personal life and on stage. We all have many different roles that we've assumed during our lifetime. We have been daughter, son, teacher, student, lover, artist, traveler, waiter, and the list goes. When we start examining those "characters" we've lived, we can begin to see which ones we've liked and which ones we haven't. For example, my first job out of high school was working as a busboy at a local cafeteria. I hated being the low man on the totem pole. In stark contrast to that, I was the "hero" in a commercial! I recently went to dinner and saw a young high-school student busing the tables next to mine, and my heart twisted into a pretzel as I looked back at how "low" myself image was back then. I would cringe at any criticism or if anyone looked at me cross. When I shot the commercial, I felt powerful, loved being the "center of attention." This game of "what roles have you played" will give you clues as to where your center of power is.

Roles I've played in my life. (Repeat this five times.)

1. Busboy (weak, broke)
2. Artistic director (powerful, assertive)
3. Husband (loved, creative)
4. Teacher (helpful, powerful)
5. Actor (strong, rich)

Now, write out how you *felt* as you played *each* one. Sometimes you'll get two different emotions that come up for you. Just trust it!

Over this week, while you are doing your "acting practice" think of your specific brand or product and start seeing ways to best market it. Do your headshots, demo reel and wardrobe reflect the "brand" that you are selling? Over the next four weeks begin to assemble these things.

Tasks

1. *Create a logline for your talent in the third person.* "Stephen Foster is a short funny younger Leslie Jordan."

2. *List your faults or honor your faults.* List ten things you don't like about yourself or your personality. How do they serve you as an actor?

3. *My "star" self.* Go through magazines and pull pictures of stars or models that you'd like to emulate. Paste them into your notebook and write about what qualities they have that you'd like to acquire.

4. *Headshot or resume inventory*: *Who do you see in your picture? What does your resume say about you?* If you are a comedian, do they say "funny"? If you are a dramatic actress, do they look like you can tackle dramatic roles? Does your resume reflect those types of characters and parts that you play best?

5. *Picture morgue.* Using your pictures, paste your "logline" on them and post them somewhere where you can see them each day. I post them on the outside of my acting notebook. You might put them on your desk, in a frame, or you might tape it to the wall by your desk. Look at it everyday and see yourself being that person.

6. *Career map.* Draw in your notebook a "map" of your success. Write down the things you want to happen along the way. (e.g., "I get signed by a great agent," "I move to New York," "a director casts me in a funny film," "I win the Oscar," etc.) You can also pull images from magazines to enhance this.

7. *Age appropriate.* How old are you? What does your "age" have to offer the acting world? What life experience have you had that make you a fascinating actor? What have you lived through that makes an interesting story for late-night talk shows. (e.g., "I'm twenty-five, and when I was little, we moved from town to town. I had to learn how to quickly adapt to the changing people, places, and things in my life. I learned how to be flexible on the ever-changing face of a theater career.")

8. *List ten things you like about yourself. How can they serve you as an actor?*

Week 9: Check-in

1. How many days did you do your "I remembers . . ."? Do you see a pattern of your life starting to evolve?
2. What script did you read? Remember that reading script gives us a ground and fills the form. Have you started to pinpoint roles you are best suited to play? Have you started to play "casting director" with some of your fellow actors?
3. Are you remembering to put images in your notebook? This week pull images of movie/tv/theater stars that remind you of yourself.
4. Have you noticed any synchronicity yet? What was it? (Did any acting opportunities come your way?)
5. Any other issues come up for you? Have you been tempted to stop acting?

Week 10
Act 3, Scene 2

If you're going to be a star, you have to act like a star . . .
I never go out unless I look like Joan Crawford, the star.
—Joan Crawford

Public and Private Self

I'm fascinated by Joan Crawford. Not because of the "Mommie Dearest" hype, but because of the fact that her entire life was built around being Joan Crawford—the movie star. She created this role of movie star and she played it to the hilt. She wanted people to know she was Joan Crawford when she strutted down the street or arrived at a party. George Cukor who directed her said he got to know all his stars personally except Joan Crawford because she never let Joan Crawford down. It was a mask, a larger than life persona that she adopted and lived with until the day she died. The audience always knew it was "Joan Crawford" playing the role. Meryl Streep, on the other hand, completely hides herself in her characters, and the public knows very little about her as a person. There are different forms of celebrity and actors.

As actors, we can often feel like two completely different people. We have our "public self" and our "private self" to contend with. Great, big movie stars often get the two confused and mixed up. Judy Garland was a great entertainer, but once the lights went off and the audience went home, she was completely troubled. Her life was built around the "public property" that was created for her at MGM, which gave little credit to the person she was. She had great difficulty leading a "grounded," stable lifestyle. It's very important for us young actors to know where the divining point is so we don't go nuts.

My "public" self is someone who is always funny, witty, and giving. I like this "character" that I have created. But my "private" self is secluded, introverted, and nerdy. I have to do a constant juggling act between the two. If I do a performance where I give a lot out to the "public," I have to do things privately to feed that other side of myself.

Think of the "public" character you are building through this workbook as a "character" that you are creating. This is your "marketing" self or your product. One of my greatest teachers said to me, "The funniest people are often the shiest ones," when I told her how "shy" I was and didn't have enough "personality" to be an actor. She was so right.

This week examine the question: Who am I to the "public" and who am I in "private"?

If you give your attention to something for as little as 17 seconds, you're on your way to creating it!
—Abraham-Hicks

Don't Engage

As you climb up the ladder of success, riches, fame, and power, you are going to ultimately come face-to-face with enemies. These can be your needy friends, your overcritical boss, coworker or the strung out family members, but some of them will be other actors! I have a fast, surefire rule that I've *always* adhered to "don't engage" when someone comes along with crisis or drama. I have learned to avoid them like the plague. Remember it's your creativity you are saving. Forget being "nice"! Their high-wire circus act can sink your creative ship!

I recently worked on a shoot, and the other actor said to me, "Why don't you stop and deliver your line right at me." And I in the moment knew he wanted me to do the scene his way so he could get a "look." I ignored him! I've learned the lesson the hard way, and I'm going to be polite as I can, but *"don't engage!"* In my past, I would have said, "Oh, let's try it!" or worse, "Okay . . . ," but I just went back to my mark and did the scene the exact way the director asked me to. I wasn't against the other actor, but I wasn't in favor of his idea, and I didn't want to get tossed from the emotion! If I were to have said anything to him, I would have sunken down into the quicksand of "actor directing actor," and I had too much work to do!

How does this relate to your career as an actor? Everything! *Everything!* Acting is dramatic, but your *life* doesn't have to be steeped in conflict, aggravation, and hatred! There are so many people, places, and things that will "temp" you away from your goal. It's difficult enough to get up on the stage or screen without the added pressure of personal troubles! When I was working on my film *Off Hollywood,* I quit my job two weeks before we started filming, just to reboot my personal computer and be a blank slate for my acting. I took that added time (along with my vacation pay) and got "normal" again. I watched TV, read books, and went to the gym so I could have a buffer of time between being a "dumb secretary" to being a "*star*." I couldn't just leap off the plate of "Stephen, send out this e-mail, get my coffee, we need more toner for the printer" to the frying pan of "Stephen, can I get *you* a cup of coffee, a tissue, and a chair." So I let myself recharge my battery to get ready!

But this "don't engage" philosophy can save you many hours (and years) of unnecessary drama and overstimulated emotion! Don't try to save the world and act! You will fail at both. When that needy client starts to chirp, just nod your head (and pretend to listen), but don't "engage" them. I screen my phone calls. I'll listen to a message to check out if someone is over-needy or in a crisis that will trump my success. I used to be an open gate of sensitivity and "engage" in everyone and everything that came across my path, but now I just walk the other way, or leave the room.

What you have to *believe* is this: *Whatever* you give your attention (and emotion) to, you'll create in *your* life! Just start talking to someone about a subject and you'll see it played out in your life! I hear actors get on the set and start complaining (yes, I've been a victim of this, too), and they make it *so* much harder for everyone! So if you're "hanging out" with worried, angry, fearful, guilty, and needy drama addicts, you'll become one yourself. And what unfortunately happens is you spend your spiritual "trust fund." It's like you give people the pin number to your god-given inheritance (ATM machine) and often you don't realize it until "it's too late!" But if you begin to pay attention to *what* people say and *how* they behave (with *strong* emotion), you'll see a direct relationship to what they have in their lives. The multimillionaire does not talk of poverty or sickness or failure. The poor talk and do things for the "poor victims" and wonder why they draw such things into *their* lives! As an actor, your job, your *only* job, is to *act* and *get paid* for it! It's got to be the obsession of all obsessions! And if you can get this *one* element liked, you'll be well on your way to winning at your game! Lately, I've been saying to friends, "If life is a game, mine's Monopoly, and I have the deed to Boardwalk and Park Place!" In fact, on my daily walk, I found a monopoly game that someone has set out on the curb and I grabbed it and used it as part of my "visualization."

It's not that I don't care, but I want to hang out with the winners because they help, and the "lemons," as my sister calls them, will only drag you down to hell and make you feel like it too! It takes extreme focus to be an actor, and it's impossible to create while you fix others, help them, or even "speak" of their drama. It's positive to have clear boundaries around yourself and know where *you* are going in your career. Those who are positive will feel good and all the others will feel bad to you.

We're bombarded with TV, e-mail, phone calls, billboards, and conversations, that we need some screening process, and when you first begin acting, you must "hibernate" and get clear about your dreams and aspirations and don't talk too much about it until after you've accomplished it. I've seen many students begin on their journey, get a good head of steam going, and then talk to one of their "lemons" and wonder why they've lost their enthusiasm and brilliance. Keep your dreams alive by doing them *first* and then use what you have left to give the world! Trust me there are many people who will put the world on their shoulders and "save" it, but right now, you concentrate on *you!*

As a friend said to me, "Give of your excess, not your essence." One student of mine who was blocked around money and couldn't pay his phone bill told me the check to the phone company bounced because he had written a good-sized "tithe" check to his church. I wanted to question, "You tithed to the church before you took care of your basics?" See, this student was in the "I'll take care of others before myself." If you don't have the dough to pay your bills, don't tithe! Give when you're in the black!

The same with emotional situations! Often, we think we can "handle" basket cases while we're working, but often it overloads the system and our circuits break and we are drained of life (acting) energy! Let's be honest, you can't do your best audition, filming, or class work while you're dealing with "Blanche DuBois" lurking around the shadows of your life. Let her be carried off to the nuthouse and move on.

So avoid the trap by not "engaging" them. But how? This can be tricky. Become sneaky. Don't tell them your "secret" plans. Draw a line in the sand. Cut them off! Find yourself a new set of "friends" and be as picky as you would if you were shopping for a home to live in. Would you pick a broken down dump with no door or window or roof to live in or would you pick a brand-new deluxe two-story mansion? Choose carefully! This point cannot be stressed enough. *You are who you hang with.* And if you personally don't know any successes, start finding them. Look in books, look in magazines, look on Facebook, do *anything* to get closer to your dream!

I recently went on what Julia Cameron calls an "Artist Date" to the Warner Brothers Studio. It's my dream to have my TV show on that studio and to occupy the offices that Bette Davis once kept. When I arrived, they had a choice of the regular tour and the "deluxe" tour. The deluxe included a meal at the commissary. Well, I had to get in there, so I paid the extra money. I said, "Well, it's expensive, but I know I'll be repaid somehow." Well, I was on the tram and got a phone call from my director of the movie I'm working on, and he said, "We resume filming on July 7," and I said, "*Yes!*" I had to in that moment *expand* so the universe could mirror that back to me! On the lot, I got to visit three sound stages, eat a fancy lunch (where all the executives of the studio eat), and make *deals* (did I mention make deals?!), and I saw exactly where Jack Warner gave Bette Davis her offices. It was the complete top floor of a building. *Hello!* The entire time, the tour guide was telling about the current TV shows, but I was in my own world. I was in the world of "someday, this is all going to be mine." I was *not* a tourist! I was being guided around the studio I most want to work in. All day long I had chills and thrills of positive expectation and belief that my series would be there very soon!

So, in this example, I hope I've shown you *how* to "not engage." Get out! Stop "talking" to them. Turn off the computer, TV, cell phone, or any noisy situation and think about your dream! As my great-grandmother used to say about people who got on her nerves, "Go about your rat killing!" So build up your fantasy life, and you'll begin to see it in your real life. It's certainly better than watching CNN or those blasted political debates!

Through the "don't engage" technique, we are learning how to detach our misplaced energies and use them to act. What? Begin to practice the art of detachment. Detachment doesn't mean you don't care. Detachment is letting go of the outcome. It's releasing the results. It's about allowing our good to flow to us. Awakening is also coming out of sleep and out of our fog and into clarity. When you are clear about something, you are free to make changes. When you are vague, you only spin your wheels.

I used to think detachment meant I didn't care. It used to drive me crazy that I cared so much about my career. I thought something was wrong with me to have an ambition toward my acting. I thought ambition was shameful and something I should feel guilty about. I guess I didn't act for so many years that when I started doing it again, I felt like I had to have ambition. But ambition became short-lived as I found that it could take me out of the love of acting—acting with passion instead of poisonous, cutthroat ambition. We don't have to beat anyone out. There is room for us all. Stop looking at the silly odds game. I had to begin blessing not only myself and my soul but the game and other opponents, knowing we could all win. There are parts out there for us all. We will win some and lose some. This is perfect. Have fun when you play this game. You'll get there. Trust yourself.

This week, take a look at these sabotaging elements and begin to free yourself from some of their negative influence in your life.

Battle vs. Game

Often we think acting must be a battle, a war, a race, when only through terrorist acts can we get to the top. I am thinking now of a play that I auditioned for when I became unblocked—I went on the audition as a dare to myself (sometimes, my inner child responds to that). We had done the show in college, and I didn't get cast. (I was the understudy and very unhappy because I knew I was the better actor.) I went to the audition as an artist date. But I had ammunition this time (the one thing I'm trying to teach in this workbook), confidence. I went to the audition, and I was dressed as the character. (Later, one of the cast members said he remembered me from the audition and knew I'd get the role.) I had dressed in blue jeans, a baseball cap, T-shirt, and sneakers. Everything the character was. It was the smallest part in the play, but I didn't care. I had to prove to myself (even if it was ten years later) that I was the right one. Well, I got the role and had a blast. So never give up! If you are right for a part, play that role even in your living room until "they" wise up and give it to you.

We want to pose as actor complaining instead of silently moving ourselves daily forward. Acting requires that we move steadily along one step at a time. Practicing day by day on our craft, we often think we have to capsize our lives in order to act. That's just drama, save it for the stage. I know I've done it. ("I can't stay in this job and go to auditions" when I didn't even have headshots, much less auditions.)

So many times the emphasis is placed on the agent, the career, marketing, showcasing, and so little attention is paid to the craft, to the fun. So often we judge ourselves so harshly that we never have any fun. Acting is fun. That's why they are called plays. The process is fun. We overlook this fact.

People always ask me, "Aren't there too many actors already?" And I say, "No." I believe that acting is as ancient and as part of our heritage as we are, and we have this screwed up belief that acting belongs to a small tribe of successful or lucky people. We forget that as children we acted quiet naturally, but often as teenagers when we tell our parents or teachers or friends, we are told to not dream so big. They give us the odds. They tell us all the reasons why we can't have what we want. If we were meant to act, then I believe we must put our attention on that just like we would put our attention on a job. But before we make the jump too high, I say begin small by making acting a priority. Make it something you enjoy rather than something you are mortally frightened of. Make friends with the fact that you want to act. Make your career a game (with a plan!) and play as well as you can. In other words, give your all before giving up!

Often we believe our success has to happen overnight. One day you're a nothing, a nobody, and then *bam!* you're world famous. That's how the headlines want us to believe. What this is really is the media hyping and not real. What "they" fail to report is all the years, months, and days before of struggle, nothings and nos before the *fame*. The work that didn't propel you to stardom or the show that got savage reviews or the small part that got cut from the film. We are trained to value ourselves as actors in terms of the success rate of our work. Leonardo DiCaprio won worldwide fame after *Titanic* launched him to our minds, but we forget all the small (and better in my opinion) roles he played before landing the box office jackpot. So what I'm hedging you toward is to judge your acting in terms of yourself. Judge your success and measure your worth on whether you showed up for the work today. Today is the only day you can create in. Tomorrow is so far away. Yesterday is out of date. Today is the only day you can count on.

We have built a hierarchy around acting. "I'm not on Broadway," we say when we are doing smaller theater. "I'm not in movies," we whine when we are making commercials or student films. Instead of using what we have on hand, we indulge in "out-there" thinking. We believe in the cultural mythology that there is important acting and not so important acting. Any acting we do (in any capacity) is acting. Acting is acting. Use whatever acting you are currently acting in to carry you over to larger avenues. We are impatient and abuse ourselves instead of being gentle and loving. Our job is to be joyful in whatever we're doing. If all the acting you are doing is in class, then that's fine. Don't judge yourself harshly for where you are.

If we aren't being cast in films or commercials, does that make our work as actors not count? No. We have build a hierarchy around acting. Acting in films is better than theater. Both forms can exist at the same time. Both have validity and both have their drawbacks. Act in your living room. Find a friend with a video camera and make your own movies. Create your own platform. We forget that we always have the power.

Acting is a lifelong learning process. We think we've got it, we understand and then we must go back to the start—beginning again, over and over. Acting is not something you get once and you never have to examine again. Actors forget this. Acting always requires risk. We must be willing to act badly, audition badly in order to one day be good. To act when we are not in the mood is a good habit to practice. Over time, we will build a foundation upon which we can stand solidly. Actors seldom let themselves act just for the pure joy of acting, for absolute pleasure. Acting is enjoyable. Acting is a risky business. We never know when or from where our break will come, but we must daily continue and endure. We must continually act on our own behalf. If we act each day, we will build up time on the stage, and this automatically makes us better—more free, happy, and joyous. We are not happy or healthy when we don't allow ourselves to act. It is always a choice. We can't determine whether or not we are cast, but we can choose to act. If we would only allow ourselves to act, the world we inhabit would be happy, more bearable. Acting practice gives us solidity in a career field that is not always solid. We don't know where or when the next door will swing open; our job is to remain in the act, to remain ready, willing, and able.

Often, we stop right when it gets going. When it looks "bad" or scary, we give up instead of pushing on, we breakdown in a heap and let "other" things overcome us. When we are this stuck, it's hard to feel free. We get suddenly concerned with the dramatics at a job or the needs of our family or the demands of our own perfectionist. We crowd our minds with "someday, I'll get to my acting . . ." and never do. Thus, we carry the weight of waiting for the right moment. In difficult times, writing helps, picking up a play and reading helps, and going to an audition for no good reason helps. At this point in your journey, it's a good idea to set small and gentle goals and meet them. Don't overburden or burn yourself out. Don't jump from the building yet. Go one story at a time, one footstep, one headshot, and one resume.

In order to practice our acting, we don't need hours of "off" time. As an actor, I must constantly feed my creative ideas. I practice my acting when I'm at the job . . . I use every chance I get to "perform" or be "on." Even when I'm in the middle of my hectic days, I am listening for bits of conversations—I'll answer the phone with a hint of English accent or I'll leave someone a message with a Southern accent. Are these forms of acting? Yes. Don't wait until you're "on the stage" to practice your craft. I listen to people's conversations for the way a character I'm working on speaks or a turn of phrase that I like. I'll be the one you see at the party in the corner watching a couple well . . . coupling. I'll stand slack jaw in a mall watching a pair of star-crossed lovers feud while the kid kicks and screams on the floor. I'll sneak into a window of a store and see a young blonde woman sucking in her stomach as she tries on a pair of too tight blue jeans. I'll stare at a man in the grocery store as he selects roses to bring home to his lover or maybe mail to his mother in the hospital. See, all of these details are not facts. I don't walk up to these people and survey them asking, "What are you doing . . . Tell me about yourself!" I let my imagination run wild. I imagine situations and then when I'm cooking up a character, I draw from these magnificent gems. I tend to think of the human race as animals in a zoo. I try as best as I can to go unobserved while I peek into their lives.

I'll walk differently just to try on another set of legs. Your body, your voice, your arms, your legs, private parts, your lips and eyes, even your emotions are your tools. You must learn to adapt and mold on them. Don't just limit them to move or turn the way you do. You are clay . . . malleable, flexible. "Should I take ballet or fencing?" I say, "Do it if you think you'll learn by it and if you'll like it!" Don't get too stuffy and rule oriented about your acting. Think of it as fun. Hard work, but don't think of it too much like a job. That can bog us down and zap our joy. We get too serious in regard to acting, thinking of it as a "career." "But don't I have to be serious?" No. You simply have to show up and do your best. The career will heat up, go stale, stall, and come back again, but the point of acting practice keeps us on point. The method of showing up and practicing is what keeps us in the game and away from the battle.

Have fun playing your acting game.

Tasks

1. *Them vs. Me*. List five times when you stopped believing in yourself due to the lack of support from others.

2. *Florence Nightingale: List ten needy people, places, and things that distract you from your path.* (Include yourself, if you should be on the list.) Why do you think you need to save them? What would happen if you left them alone?

3. *List ten people who you think have it "going on!"* Those who seem put together, have ambition, and money. You might only know *one*, that's okay, it's a start. What do they have that you *want*? And if you don't know them personally, try to get in their "circle" mentally!

4. *Change of scenery: Change your "look."* Dramatically, alter your hair, your wardrobe, and your makeup. Notice the reactions during the week. Do you pull back when someone offers their "critique"? Have one of your friends take some snapshots of your altered look. Keep these images in your acting notebook.

5. *Public and private self.* Describe in your notebook the difference between your "public" and your "private" self.

6. *Life game*. Describe your career as a "game" that you like. Is it "*Risk,*" "*Clue,*" "*Old Maid,*" "*Bingo*"? "*Atari.*" (I threw that one in to make you laugh.)

Week 10: Check-in

1. How many days did you do your "I remembers . . ."? Have you mentioned them to a fellow actor yet?
2. What script did you read? Have you found yourself excited by a character or a scene yet and started to find a way to film it or act it in some form?
3. Are you remembering to put images in your notebook? Have you put images in of awards you want to win, roles you want to play, or reviews you're going to get? Seeing is believing.
4. Have you noticed any synchronicity yet? What was it? (Did any acting opportunities come your way?)
3. Any other issues come up for you? Have you been tempted to stop acting?

Week 11
Act 3, Scene 3

Natural Talent vs. Trained Talent

Everyone has natural talents. Some actors who are naturally gifted and have a flair for the dramatic are often stifled and bottled up. Sort of like the gene inside the bottle. All that is required is to remove the cap. When I tell my students that I was the shiest wallflower all through school—the kid who hid in the corner—they are shocked. They don't know the long, upward struggle it took for me to be "born." I worked very hard at transforming my "natural" talent into a marketable skill. It took me a long time to bust out of my shell and understand my comedy was my divine gift. What I did best. My partner Chuck calls this "core competence" or what you are extremely gifted at doing without struggle.

For all practical purposes, I was not "born" to be an actor. I had crooked teeth, I had a high-pitched girly voice, I was short (five feet tall), and I had no role models or family encouragement to act. Acting was as far away from my family circle as multimillionaires. My family had no knowledge of acting or what it meant or that you could have a career at it. But something inside of me told me that I could. In Ruth Gordon's autobiography, she talks about hearing her voices to go on the stage while at a performance of Hazel Dawn. I guess I've always had the same hunch. The one thing my family did have was a flair for comedy. They could make the craziest remarks out of the most trivial things, and they also had a flair for high drama. Maybe that environment was perfect for me to flourish in, in retrospect. I wanted my mom to be like Mamma Rose in *Gypsy* and push me onto the stage, but she certainly was not that and I had to learn how to do it on my own: trial and error, success and failure!

In ninth grade, I got my first real "hunch" about acting as a possible "career." I took a stagecraft class and thought I'd work backstage: painting flats, getting props, prompter, and publicity. In that class, our teacher made us sign a contract for a grade. Your grade in the class was based on how much work you did. I took to it like a duck to water. It was a difficult time for my family: My dad was away in Okinawa and my sister got pregnant, and I stayed after school in the theater department. The theater became my escape from reality and my spiritual connection. I did not know what was being formed inside of me. The first time I auditioned was for a play was the musical *Runaways,* and they had everyone audition, it was part of the class. And I showed up, and all the other kids knew how to audition and sang like birds. When it was my turn, I stood in front of the piano, and the choir teacher played the beginning of "Happy Birthday" and I did not know when to come in and completely messed up. I was in front of all these kids singing! It was hell! He looked at me like I was a helpless freak. I sang the song once more completely out of tune, and he wrote "tone-deaf" on the audition paper and told me to sit down. It broke my heart. I wanted to sound like Olivia Newton-John. So I did work backstage while I learned all I could about theater. I remember staying hour and hour after school painting poster board after poster board saying "Come See Runaways."

I remember the first day of class, the kids in the class all knew each other from the year before, and there I sat in the corner all by myself: I remember how "theatrical" and larger than life they were. Shawna Surprise was the plump girl who knew everybody and was the theater department's maven! She told stories about *Oliver* and *Godspell* they had done the year before. I just wanted to fit in. I was a complete wallflower. In someways I felt like this make believe world was realer than my real "home".

As part of our grade, we all had to prepare a scene for our final. I was out sick the day we picked acting partners, and I got "stuck" with the other queer in class, Richard! Richard was a very kind guy, but everyone in the class called him names. He had a lisp and had very fey mannerisms. I felt sorry for him, but was thankful they did not single me out like that!

But we found a great scene from *The Winslow Boy,* and I played the boy and he played the inspector who interrogates a kid who stole stuff from another kid's locker. I prepared my part, learned all my lines by rote, and we rehearsed it and rehearsed it! Well, the day came and we put our little scene up on the stage, and we get two lines into the scene and he goes up! He stared at me blankly and whispered, "Stephen, I forgot my lines," and I thought I'd croak right there. I knew nothing about improv or acting, and I just sat there staring at him. He was supposed to ask my character questions, and I had all the responses. He then stage-whispered again, "Go to the end, Stephen!" And so I broke down in fake hysterics and said, "I didn't do it. I wasn't there," throwing my head dramatically down on the table. And then the most awful thing happened, he suddenly remembered his *lines! Hello!* And in the middle of my dramatic moment, he says, "So where were you at 7:45 p.m.?" I could have killed him. We muddled through the rest of the scene, and I did another breakdown and we got off the stage quickly!

The teacher had all the students write comments on each scene, which we got the next day and Richard, and I read ours together and they said very nice things about me, but Richard's comments were just awful. They attacked his lisp, and some even called him names. I felt so sorry for him, but I was happy that they liked me. But I thought that if I lived through that, I might stand a chance at acting, but it still took me long, long years to make it to the point where I called myself an actor.

I remember my first camera audition when I was so scared that I didn't have a grain of personality. I just stood there and weakly smiled a faint smile like the sixth-grade school pictures. I walked out of that casting office vowing, "I'll never give a dead audition again!" What do I mean by "dead"? It's not a judgment or indictment, but a way of looking at my acting so I could get better. After that, I would do anything to get a reaction out of the casting directors. If I didn't get the role, I made damned sure I was noticed. They would remember me.

Natural talent is about trusting your instincts and going out on a limb every time. Children when playing have natural acting abilities because they play "make-believe" a lot until they are told to grow up and get serious. They believe in their fantasies and make-believe and games until they are told they are meaningless and not adult. Actors are no different. We rely on that sacred world of make-believe. We need those fantastic, outrageous fantasies, but we try to squander our frivolity, thus we create flat, boring, and diluted lives and performances.

The trained actor can fall into the trap of being too trained, too rehearsed, and too rigid. Sometimes, they have to become untrained in order to become unblocked. When you go to a movie or play, you don't want to say, "Oh, he does good Meisner or Method." You want to believe the character, the circumstances, not the school the actor studied at.

In order to act, we have to give certain behaviors up. This sounds cutthroat, and it is. Acting requires that we give it our attention. Acting requires more attention than other arts because it can easily slip by us. Acting is not only about auditions, sitcoms, pilot seasons, and being on Broadway. Acting is staying true and staying in the game. Acting is noticing our habits, getting rid of them, and replacing them with healthy ones. Giving up our old former behaviors can be tricky. Sometimes, we aren't even aware we have habits until we take an honest look at our lives. When we can see what is "blocking" us, we can begin to make progress in releasing them. So much of what blocks us is internal as well as external.

Acting is a game you must play to win. Don't be indifferent about your acting. Speak in bold terms. Not, "I did okay." Okay doesn't convey much feeling. Feeling is "I did the greatest or I fell right on my face!" This is better. Feel fierce in your acting. Make the game something you are actively involved in, not numbly detached from. Instead of saying, "Damn them! I am the best actor in the world! I deserve the role!" and keep preparing material or sending headshots out, we say, "I feel okay. It doesn't hurt . . . Oh, well . . ." and we stop rolling the dice. When you don't nail it, raise the stakes! Roll the dice again. Get back on the game board.

Know what you're worth and stick to it. Make your mind up that you were born to act and keep moving. "Never give up!" Ruth Gordon said. Trust her, she should know. Remember this: while you have stopped, others are still moving. Movies are still being shot, plays are being cast, and commercials are being done. Never give up.

One of the myths we commonly hold is there is such a thing as "real" or "serious" acting and playing around doesn't count. It does count. Acting occurs in the moment. Actors act. I hate to break this to you. The difference between actors who don't act and those who do comes with the doing. If you're practicing acting, you are acting. We think we have to be getting paid for it or applause for it to count. Don't wait to get paid or even when you are in class. Act all the time. Act when you are at the job, act when you are on the bus, act in the middle of your love life, act while you are driving to work. Acting can be done anywhere, anytime. When you go for that important job interview, practice your entrances.

Acting does not stop when we leave the stage. Acting is always going on. Acting is living. I used to divide my life into neat, orderly sections. I have my real life over here and my acting life over here; I have my writing life over here, I have my love life over here . . . they were like pieces of pie that I had to be in the mood to eat. "Oh, today, I feel like an actor, so I do actor things. Or today, I feel like a writer, so I do writer things . . ." Acting and writing can be integrated into our lives in healthy doses.

An acting career requires both commitment and enthusiasm. It's good that we create a good relationship with our acting lives. In a sense, we must enjoy and persist in our careers. Acting is a business where one can grow easily discouraged and pull back the reins and stop altogether. This workbook and "acting practice" are aimed at arming ourselves against self-attack, about pushing on and surviving the falls, the failures, and advancing despite the odds and the obstacles. Over any length of time, we can heal our old wounds, break patterns and rebuild, and rehab our lives and careers.

There are sometimes when I don't want to act, when I don't want to write, and I'll go to any length to avoid it. I've learned to be very gentle and vigilant with myself. When I'm resistant, I look at what I'm feeling about a circumstance in my life, and I try to gently show up at my acting practice.

Often, when we are blocked as actors, we spend swaths of our time and energy feeding that block giving "being blocked" the attention it doesn't deserve. In short, we give it too much airplay. As actors, we don't give ourselves due credit. We don't look clearly at the good steps we've taken. Instead, we look at all the thing we've not accomplished or attempted or what we still have to do. This is very damaging and dangerous to our creative child. All the child wants to do is act. Acting is a process of committed actions. "Today, I commit to do X, Y, and Z" and sticking to it. Don't concern yourself with yesterday or tomorrow, work only in and on today. This gives you a solid ground to build a career. It's difficult to build a solid house when you keep cutting off your hand with the buzz saw or building the roof before you have the walls completed or the foundation laid. Acting is allowing. What we are after is letting ourselves build slowly and surely. We can only trust ourselves when we have something trust. What we can trust is acting practice. The minute you step away and set aside your drama or melodrama, you are free to create. And acting feels magical and inspired again.

The more you perform, the more experience you get, the better you get at it. Now, there is the way that some actors go: They skim the surface of what they want or they stand in the sidelines while time goes by waiting (on tables) for their *big break* instead of pushing through.

Acting became magical for me because every night I would perform I'd be in a trance and enchanted by acting. As actors, we have to return to that place where we play. Acting is playing. But we think of acting as something we only do for a living and we consider it our jobs and we rob ourselves from the pure joy and glee of it. Acting is just another way of looking at or viewing life. Acting is an art form and a business. The creation of acting is free.

We begin to awaken from within because that is where the imagination is fertile. We start within and then it manifests without. We first catch a glimpse of our idea in the mind's eye and then we seek without to bring it to life. There is a great deal of time and energy spent on the externals of our careers that we forget what we are truly intrigued and inspired by. We see first what we want and then find out how. We grasp what is impossible and make it possible.

I tend to think of acting in terms of what I put into it, I usually get out. I send my headshots out just to keep in circulation. I write letters to keep the energy out and to keep myself focused. With the invention of the Internet, we now have new avenues from which to empower ourselves. We can market ourselves in new ways. This is good. Don't fear technology, use it. I got some of my best bookings from being active online. If things are going to aid you, let them. Keep your headshots out in the world. Send them out with affirmations: "These headshots are now being seen by the right people." "I am always in the right place at the right time." "My headshots are now landing in the proper hands." This thought also applies to flyers and other forms of advertisements. Know that whatever marketing you do, it will lead somewhere.

You are a traveling salesman when it comes to your acting career. You never know who is going to help you or what door will suddenly appear before you. Carry your headshots, business cards, demo reels, and postcards with you at all times. I met a friend in a coffee shop I was working at. He was the only "professional" writer I knew at the time, and I constantly said to him, "Write a part for me!" Over time, we became friends, and he wrote a short film for me and helped me develop a TV show. So always be on the alert for help along your trail.

We are afraid to act on full throttle. We have some pretty grim reason and excuses we make instead of devoting our hearts and souls to acting. This is a sense of withdrawal and dispassion. Passion is a fuel. Even when there seems to be no work, the agent hasn't called, and we look crazy for sticking with such a foolish business, if we have our hearts into it, those things don't really matter to us. We love it.

I learned that I have to be willing to be a failure as an actor, that didn't mean I wasn't concerned with success; that would be lying. I always wanted success since I was a little kid in front of the TV set in Fort Worth, Texas, watching Carol Burnett doing her wild characters. Some part of me said, "I can do that." What I mean by I had to fail was, I had to keep jumping into the lake of creativity. I had to continually keep risking.

Become a portable actor. Act all the time. We do this on a subconscious level. Be a traveler. Act wherever you go. Acting doesn't have to be reserved for the stage or when you're cast in a commercial or film or stage play. "Keep your channel open," dancer Martha Graham tells us. One of the games I play with myself is that I'm always giving an audition. This keeps me turned on and heated up. I feel more alert, more sharp when I pretend that everything I do is an audition.

I hear actors say, "I need to get new headshots!" They say this in exasperation and frustration. I tell them to use the ones (yes, the ugly ones with your bad hair!) until they get new ones. "But they are terrible!" They shoot back. "So what!" Don't wait until you get new ones before you take the action to mail them out. It's just a head game actors play with themselves. If you mail them out until you run out, you might get a job and then you can afford to get your better headshots. Remember it's a numbers game. Keep your face in circulation.

Using the Day Gig Blues

I was on a film shoot recently, and I was talking to a man who was twenty-eight and just getting started. He listed all the "jobs" he had done since coming to Los Angeles. "I've been a car salesman, a real estate salesman, a restaurant manager . . . ," and it reminded me of how easy it is to place our jobs as the priority. I've learned from painful experience that I use my job as another way that I avoid taking risk as an actor. I recall auditions I didn't go on because the boss wouldn't let me. I remember at one point, I gave up acting and settled into a real job. I did this until my soul about exploded.

Use those jobs as a way to propel your creative career and not hinder it. I find a lot of actors think that one day some magical person is going to swoop down into the office or restaurant and recognize their wonderful service and give them a contract. Hardly. Don't fall into the day job trap and wait to act. We tend to think that acting is not a real job. It is. I'll say it again. Acting is a real job! In my experience, acting demands all the attention and commitment of any day job that I've held. Acting is work. We only discount it because we enjoy doing it. I used to think there was something "wrong" with me because I didn't enjoy working at jobs besides acting. It took me a very long time to come to realize that it just wasn't my soul's path to work in an office or restaurant. I remember I went through a period of thinking: "If only I had a job in the industry . . ." until the light bulb went off that said, "Stephen, you're full of it! You don't want that. You want an acting job." This flash of honesty woke me up. It startled me at first because I thought I could work my way into acting. I also find it funny and sad that actors can pretend to do any job. Of course, we can. We are good actors! I pretended I was a receptionist for an entire year while I waited for the finances of the film *Off Hollywood* to come back together.

The question became: Why won't I put my heart and soul into acting the way I did everything I didn't like to do? Why was I such a slave to the life I didn't want and so unwilling to follow what I thought would make me tremendously happy? How could I ignore my true destiny? Was it my birthright to be so unlucky? So miscast in a life that fit like a suit I had grown out of? What would happen if I pursued my dreams? What if I listened to my inner guidance (and I thought my inner guidance was just a foolish longing)? And lastly, why did I postpone with such panache my acting career? The stories of me as a weak and helpless sprang immediately into my mind. The end of my story had me broke and crazy not successful and rich (although that is what I felt I had inside!). I had to do some examining of myself, some soul-searching, some ironing out of what I thought acting actually was.

When to Stop Paying Dues

Knowing when to spend your money and when not to can be a very confusing subject, and when you, do you *stop* paying dues? Or when do *you* get paid for acting?

It's dangerous to spend a fortune on your acting career. Joining theater companies where you have to pay monthly dues and in enrolling in casting director workshops and seminars can do two destructive things: drain your finances and make you feel like you're not getting anything out of it but poor. Having artistic hunger does not mean financial poverty and you don't have to spend excess amounts of money on your career. Some very nice headshots and a demo reel will do.

I started to make money at my career when I said definitely, "Universe, I put my foot down! I've spent ten years of throwing my money at this and *now* I need to demonstrate some *paid* acting gigs!" And I got paid for doing the show *Come Back to the Five and Dime, Jimmy Dean, Jimmy Dean,* two unexpected stand-up comedy gigs, and then a movie. Okay, that's the nice way I put it. The other way was "if anyone gets paid at this, it's *me!*" And I stood by it. It's a bit tricky because there are so many courses, lectures, and teachers who want you to pay them. It's like a get-rich-quick scheme: "Break into commercials. Meet casting executive at CBS . . ." I spent over $1,000 one year, enrolling in a series of casting director workshops and then a class where I knew more than the teacher.

There is another danger I want to bring to your attention and that is the casting director workshops. I'll be blunt. It's how they make a living, and to be honest, I don't believe they offer much good advice in terms of *actually* getting you work or offering anything in the way of acting tips. The majority of them have not studied acting, and became casting directors because they "knew" someone or became an assistant and worked their way up the chain. Or worse, they are failed actors. They are not there to teach or to inspire actors, but to pick up a meal ticket. And they do this night after night all over town and rarely take any time with actors. They have you do the scene, smile politely, and maybe give you an adjustment, and then add your picture to their bulging stack of headshots.

I know this is *not* a polite essay! I don't know many actors who get auditions this way. Get in however you can, but going this route can feel like doing extra work where you're treated like a number. Rise above it! It gets to feeling like you're begging for work.

Often, an actor will do very solid work, and the casting director will say something stupid just to give "feedback," but it's usually vague or worse critical. I once had a casting director tell me, "You only have a 1 percent of getting work!" Well, that's 1 percent is more than he'll ever get from me. And a casting director never knows what makes one actor succeed and another not. There is no formula for success except work. That's the problem the casting directors claim to know things and can give you secret tips to get "in". They don't have that much power. The casting director of *Off Hollywood* did not want to cast me as he did not think I could carry a feature film although my resume said I had carried tons of theater productions. The director is the one who hired me.

It can seem like throwing pennies down a well, and we keep wishing, hoping, and dreaming and that some day never seems to come and it can cost you a fortune. It's like casting your pearls ($) before swine (snort, snort, snort) and you can get pretty muddy and beaten up in the exchange.

I took a stand-up comedy class once and hated every minute of it. The teacher was a novice and teaching a "formula" for doing stand-up comedy. On the first day of class, he asked us which stand-up comics we admired, and I said, "Bette Midler," and he told me that Bette Midler was not a comedian. I knew we were *not* going to get along and should have asked for my money back. During the six weeks, I was dragged through hell with this man as each "joke" I turned out, he didn't approve of or "get." He wanted me to say things that were against my nature. I muddled through the class, and when we had our performance, the audience loved my material. I put this essay into the mix to tell you not to be tossed by those workshops and classes. I have a philosophy that I have learned, and I hope it helps you. "Unless a teacher is 100 percent for me and my success, I don't sign up!" As actors, we have a tendency to give our talents away because we so want to please the teacher.

So when it comes to picking mentors, teachers, and gurus, please make sure you are choosing the ones who are right for *you* and who *believe* in your talents. Don't pick someone who treats you like a number or like "another actor."

Reviews and Agents

Along the trail to our careers there are some things that will knock us down if we are not careful to safeguard ourselves. The first one is reviews. We will hopefully go on from "practice" to building a body of work, and we can be shot down by "bad reviews." When I first started acting, I thought I could withstand the negative comments that were written about me and my work. I can't. I am very sensitive. I was once cast in a play, and the reviewer at the *Los Angeles Times* did not agree with me being cast in the role and complained about that fact instead of reviewing my performance. This hurt. I've also had reviews that were blistering and scathing. I've learned the hard way to *not* read them. Even a wishy-washy review can send an actor into the tailspin of "what did they mean by that?" Or "this is not accurate" but it's in print, and we often believe it determines our value as actors. It doesn't.

What I do with reviews? I'll tell friends to read them for me, and if it's glowing about me, I'll read it. If it says anything negative, I don't. Some actors like to know the good, the bad, and the ugly, but not me. I want to be lifted up, not deflated.

The next item is agents. Agents are there to get you work and get money for that work. They are not there to "groom" you into stars. They can help. Agents are people you want to have a good relationship with. You want your agent to work for you so you do all you can on your end. A lot of actors complain that their agent isn't sending them out while they hang out at the local coffee shop. They don't look for any work outside of what their agent sends them on. This is dangerous for actors. We must always be looking for jobs. Even when we are cast in a role, we must be on the hunt for the next one.

Actors tend to have an adversarial approach to their agent instead of doing their work as actors (mailing, classes, networking, etc.). My agent seems to do more for me when I do more for myself. Your agent might be sending you out and you may not be getting called in at the moment. Try not to blame your agent, but you will anyway. Get those headshots out there, put your demo online, and film little scenes with your camera. And if your agent is "dead" for you, begin to shop around for another one.

Tasks

1. *"What I really want to do is act, but what I do is . . ."* Start with the sentence above and list all the things in your life you do that are *not* acting.

2. *Daily inventory* Make a daily list of everything you showed up for *today*. Give yourself some credit for even the smallest action taken in the direction of your career.

   1. Did the dishes.
   2. Got resumes copied.
   3. Helped friend retype his cover letter.
   4. Wrote on my new play.
   5. Did task from "Awakening."

3. *My dream agent.* In your notebook, list qualities you'd like to have in an agent. (Hardworking, persistent, connected, gets me lots of auditions, etc.) This week start to imagine this person in your life.

4. *My tools.* What do you have at your fingertips to advance your career? Write in your notebook the things that you have already that you can begin using: I have headshots, I have a resume, I have a computer, I have a car, I have a demo reel, etc.

5. *What I* need? In your notebook, write down a list of ten items that you need to further your career. I need better headshots, I need a manager, I need a part that is a standout, I need more money, I need an assistant, etc. (This is ordering from the universe.)

6. *Ask for help.* Find someone who you can "pray" with. This is someone who supports you and your acting career. You read your list of "needs" (from the task above) and let them read their list and then say out loud, "I see you getting a perfect manager." Meet each week either in person or online and tell each other of your progress.

7. *Reviews*. Read through any reviews that you have gotten in your career and "pull quotes." Type out these quotes and paste them in your notebook.

Week 11: Check-in

1. How many days did you do your "I remembers . . ."? Have you seen how exciting your own life has been? Do you see your life as rich material yet?
2. What script did you read? Remember that reading a script gives us a ground and fills the form. Have you let yourself really read some risky scripts?
3. Are you remembering to put images in your notebook? This week pull images of things you want to buy your actor (new headshots, demo reel, courses, vacations, and books) Seeing is believing.
4. Have you noticed any synchronicity yet? What was it? (Did any acting opportunities come your way?)
5. Any other issues come up for you? Have you been tempted to stop acting?

Week 12
Act 3, Scene 4

Trust the "Process"

Never "text" your performance in.
Give 100% 100% of the time!
—C. Stephen Foster

Acting is a spiritual practice. Actors are a part of an ancient tribe. We should act together just for the joy of doing it. Acting is a way to connect with our power, and our spiritual power as well. Acting is a way to alter the chemicals in the body. Acting has a force behind it. When we act, there is something bigger, larger than us moving us, directing us, guiding us. Actors think in terms of being a "working" actor and often get confused thinking it is a "job," and we approach it only in monetary terms—"What will this get me?" Or "when will this pay off?" instead of creating the best character to serve the script. Acting is a form of service. We serve the script, we serve the director, we serve our fellow actors, we serve ourselves, and we serve the world. But we forget this. We believe we have to be tough, harsh, bitter, competitive, and trample over people. No, we don't. This is a lie to keep us from helping one another. We must learn how to help each other. Actor to actor we must return to the spiritual truth that we are in this together. There are plenty of parts and plenty of places to act. But it's our ego that wants to remind us that there are limits. Our ego wants instant results—a one-way ticket to fame and riches instead of the steady, constant steps toward it.

Actors must continually go back to the start—another scene, another play, and another film. You must not be afraid to start over. Acting is a series of beginnings. There is power in this knowledge. This empowers us. Actors tend to forget this. Even each performance, we must go back to the start. After each take in a movie, we have to return to mark one and do it again fresh, vital, and filled with energy. This is how we add freshness to a character. Even in this course you'll go over things again and again. It's essential and often difficult to admit.

Just like writers must go back to the first word, the first sentence, and the first paragraph, actors must go back the same way—readings, auditions, plays, and films. We go back to ourselves as the canvas on which we paint. What does the character want? Who am I? In life, we continually go back to the start when we create—the new job, this cup of coffee, this relationship, etc.—all new, all fresh. The problem arises when we approach it from a sense of rote—a remoteness, a numbness, or a lesser than attitude (altitude).

Trusting ourselves is power, not an ego-based power but a sureness based on the work that we have built, a power of faith. There is also a feeling of accomplishment when we trust ourselves. Through the use of acting practice and the tools in this course, you have begun to build a body of work. This is how trust is built. Trust is built when we give ourselves something solid to stand on. Acting practice is solid. We don't wake up one morning and immediately know how to act. We have to learn how to trust our acting so that, no matter what happens in the outside world to us and our careers, we keep traveling on. We learn to trust the process of acting. We begin to sense that these higher forces are working things out for us as we learn to make one attempt after the other.

Can't regret, what I did for love.
—"A Chorus Line"

By learning to trust acting, you begin to develop a strong sense of who you are and what you truly want. You've also begun to forge a new future for yourself. You have played with scenes, you have written pages of "I remembers . . . ," and have read at least eleven scripts. All these seemingly meaningless things have guided you step-by-step back to your true calling. You don't know what will happen in the future, but you are at least prepared for it. You have tools you can always return to and utilize. There is no real end to the process of acting. Even though this is the final chapter, the final "take" in the book, it's not the end, but a beginning.

The first courageous thing to do is live. Living through life's cycles can be difficult and exhilarating. We must learn to be with it all. And staying present is challenging. Of course, this is true. Life when lived ordinarily can throw us off course. We can be blinded and tempted by all these normal everyday events as things to stop us from acting. It's my experience that these things encourage me to act. If you are courageous in your life and live with boldness, that's exactly how you'll approach acting.

When I am completely downtrodden, distressed, I read biographies of people who have made it. This cheers me up and gives me strength. I also send out e-mails and letters to friends. I also read old good reviews. I do anything to avoid getting stuck. I do a quick "I remember . . ." I read a script. I pretend I'm being cast in a movie. I visualize my dreams coming true. I take a walk. All of these you have also learned how to do through this workbook. If you have not made as much progress as you would have wised in twelve weeks, that's fine. Remember, you are after progress, not perfection. You can always circle back through the book or form a creative team around it and work the tools together.

The Eye of the Tiger

It takes great amounts of courage to go after your acting dreams. Sometimes, the only courage that gives you strength is "showing up." Letting it all fall apart sometimes means something better can be built. Sometimes, we need an earthquake in our lives to keep us moving. This takes courage. It takes courage to face the stage with only three people in the audience. It takes courage to get into your costume and mutter your lines on stage. It takes courage to face the callback. It takes courage to face the commercial auditions again. This is how you learn how to act. We don't learn so much from the successes but from the failures. From the times when we had no courage, but we kept ourselves moving along that creates endurance. It's like playing a game of Monopoly and your luck has vanished and you feel discouraged. Discouragement has the word "courage" within it. "Courage" is always inside of you, even if it's just the size of a mustard seed. That seed can be replanted and grown again. Sometimes, it takes great courage to find that courage.

"I think it's a group of insiders," a student said to me regarding making it in Hollywood. This kind of thinking must be examined and discarded. It will constantly keep you in the back of the line. Sort of like there's a private party being held to which we are not cordially invited. This type of thinking is typical, reinforced, encouraged and keeps us out of action. We don't like to believe that we are connected children of the universe. We also hold the keys to all we want, but we have to know that if we depend on others to invite us to the party, we might never get in. Get out there and start to make those connections and contacts one by one, and soon, you'll be the one hosting the parties.

Nobody is going to discover you while you are just "dreaming" of being an actor. Joan Crawford said, "I established myself in an apartment, poked my chin out to there, and allowed that one of us, either the movies or I, had to give." What this means is that you have to have a determination, a will, and a burning desire to act. Actors are made, not born.

"The universe doesn't give us things when we want . . ." according to my friend Joe. "Sometimes, it comes a day late, sometimes it comes when we least expect it, but it will come." Sometimes, the universe gives us time off from people, places, and things in order for us to come into some clarity around issues we ignore. Time off to rebuild ourselves. Sometimes, that is the gift of not getting what we want *when* we want it. It's in those times we have to take conscious stock of where we've been and all we've done. On difficult days, it's hard to see the length of the road we've traveled or the heights we've made up the mountain. It's on these days, that we must call our supportive friends, not to save us but to tell us it's all going to be okay, because we are good people, because they see our talents and believe in them. In essence, they see what we harbor in darkness. In this society, we've gotten so accustomed to doing it all by ourselves that we forget that we are a part of the community. We so quickly call needing someone "codependent" and we spend time calling ourselves names that we forget that needing friends and being vulnerable to this fact makes us strong, makes us lovable, not weak and powerless. In times of adversity, count your blessings, count your lucky stars, count your breathing, and say "thank you, thank you, thank you."

On the "off" days, it's required that we surround ourselves with these things to make us happy. Listen to the music that cheers you up. When I feel "troubled," I listen to Karen Carpenter until I feel "right" again. When I was working on the movie *Off Hollywood,* I had a support system I called "The Triumphant Triangle" consisting of Chuck, Julie, and Amy. I would call them daily from the set and would report my work to them, and they cheered me on.

WEEK 12, ACT 3, SCENE 4

Flipping the Switch (I See Dead People!)

All great actors possess a sixth, perhaps even a seventh, sense. They are able to convey to an audience what they are thinking and feeling no matter what words they happen to be speaking. Conversely, they are able to judge accurately the temper and the reactive power of the audience from moment to moment. It is as though they can tell what the audience is thinking and feeling, and then adapt their performance to match it.
—Garson Kanin from "Hollywood"

I've been saving this tool for the last, because it's the strongest, fastest way to "connect." "It came out of the blue," "I saw my life clearly," and "I see dead people," any of these statements are words I've often expressed being witness to miracle after miracle in my life once I left my troubled twenties behind! It seems like the older I get, the more I sense something "larger" happening in my life and my place in it.

When I am acting, I call upon higher spiritual hands to help me. I call upon the following troops to guide me when I'm about to perform: Judy Garland (I like how she seemed magic and had a photographic memory! I use this wonderful artist when I'm not sure of my lines and when I need to *shine!*), Groucho Marx (he shares my birthday, and I consider him the "king of comedy," and I call upon his gift of being funny in different ways: physical, punch lines, and double takes), Ruth Gordon (she had the determination of a hummingbird and deep concentration), Bette Davis (I call upon her energy of being a bit hardheaded and getting exactly what she wants. When I was working on my first feature, I actually used to drive by Warner Brothers lot just to "feel" her, and once I even went to her grave and prayed for courage), I call upon my departed father Clinton Stephen Foster (I ask him to get the laughter rolling for me if I'm about to do a stand-up gig. I ask him to tell the audience to love me as he does.), Napoleon Hill and Clement Stone (who wrote *Success Through a Positive Mental Attitude*. I call upon them for help in "selling myself" and converting each adversity into a benefit for *me!*), and recently, Orson Welles (who was a brilliant actor, writer, and director who had vision and passion. I want his focus and resolution). When I feel pressured in my personal life, I'll call upon my great-grandmother (she was grounded, loving, compassionate, and would *never* criticize me, *never!*) and her son, my grandfather (he gave up playing the viola when he was five years old because of stage fright and was a very "shy" man. I often think I act for *him!* I pray for his gift of humor. He made fun of everyone and everything. It was handed down!)

This process helps me "gather" the courage. I have many times felt this "out of body" experience while acting or writing. It is channeled! The ego blocks it and wants to claim credit when I *know* I've done my best work, when I'm doing nothing but letting the "spiritual forces" work through me. Even my years of playing dress up and doing drag, I felt as if "they" would say things that I wouldn't do. It made playing Judy Garland, Bette Davis, and Liza Minnelli fun. I thought I was just fooling around, but in retrospect, I found that I was actually "channeling" them. I was using a part of their energy to "act" through me. They were these higher frequencies that I could tap into and use in my acting.

I discovered that there are always two sides of me when I'm onstage. First, the performer performing the show, always aware of the technical elements. ("Now, I have to cross, hit my mark, and confront him.") Second, my higher spiritual self. "Oh, I should hold for laughs. They didn't get that joke . . . Get them on the next scene." That part of me is constantly alert to and watching the show.

There is an energy that passes through me when I'm acting. I used to say that I don't remember what I do onstage . . . Something takes over me making me "larger" than I am—more funny, more eager to please, more spontaneous, and more free.

I will often close my eyes and go into a deep breathing and I'll sense them one by one and feel their energy surround me, and while I'm acting, I let them "work" through me. I flip the switch "on," and they come through me and often surprise me when I'm acting. I find that "Stephen" leaves the building and these forces work through me. The moment I enter on the stage, I am in the palms of something greater. I become the channel from which the work flows. But it is built on structure and practice. This channel can become constricted if not used properly. Or we can "channel" the wrong elements of those we choose to draw from. I've known many people who have played "Judy Garland" and have attracted her darker qualities to them instead of her performing gifts. Remember, you are seeking out the *"best"* that these artists can give.

I recently was working with a student, Amy, on this, and she called upon Judy Garland to help her with her audition monologue, and she said that not only did she feel Judy but she also got Carole Lombard and Jean Harlow, and they "sorta popped in" while she was performing and a great big dog came bounding up to her with his tongue wagging right before she went into the room. This dog reminded her of Judy Garland's infectious bounding loving energy. She told me she aced the audition.

This takes a lot of tuning in, and you can't do it if you're all wound up and worried! It's like turning a radio knob and picking up the vibes of those who are gone. But they don't even have to be dead for you to tune in! You can ask for guidance from those who are living! I often tune into Madonna's fiery "I Will Do It" energy when I'm faced with a challenging hurdle or obstacle that looms too large for me! And almost as soon, as I ask, I'm given that courage and confidence.

I also use music to pick up their higher vibrations. I will put my iPod into my ears and turn on one of them until I can feel their vibes all around me. I will also write down on a piece of paper the name of the person and what I'd like them to help me with. There are many books that explore "channeling" in further detail, but for now, just asking for their help will get you some spiritual assistance.

This technique might strike you as crazy and foolish! I remind you that acting is not rational or normal, and once you try it, you'll see it work.

"Acting Is Interacting"

I was having lunch with the director of *Off Hollywood*, and we were talking about acting, and he said the most astonishing thing to me, "Acting is interacting." That to me summed up *everything* about acting. Acting is taking everything we've been handed and using it for the scene and our acting careers as well.

We as actors have been bombarded with the slogan "Acting is *reacting*," which always leaves me feeling I should wait until the other actor speaks, and do a "bit" and say my line. We often hear, "Acting is listening," which leaves me cranking my neck and staring intently at the other actor.

But "Acting is interacting" implies an interlocking of character with objects and people while moving through the time and space of the script. "Interacting" gives us the space to move around in. We interact with our scene partners; we interact with the scrub brush, the table cloth, or the zipper on our dress. When we are "interacting," we are engaged fully in the moment of the piece. Nothing is tossed out. Nothing matters but the character and the self-conscious actor disappears.

Interacting implies interlocking pieces of a puzzle that moment by moment add up to the entire whole of a performance. You interact more intensely at different times and with different people. The way I interact with my mother is entirely different than the way I interact with my agent. The way I interact with my students is entirely different to the way I interact with the bartender. The way I interact with my computer is different with how I interact with my car. Each one is specific. Each relationship to each object or character becomes something you can *play*.

"Interacting" means using all of those elements to your *best* advantage. I think it's the long forgotten intention behind acting. "Interacting" means you become this flexible, movable character rather than an actor fixed in one spot.

"Interacting" means you also enjoy the dance and the mystery of an acting career. You move with the river as you forge ahead. You enjoy interacting with others as you continue this never-ending process of acting. Acting process has taught you to hang tough, to show up, and to stay focused. If you don't get the part today, you'll get another one tomorrow. If you get dropped by your agent, the universe will supply you a better one. Your movie goes over budget, you file bankruptcy, your best friend turns sour on you, or your beloved aunt dies, you interact with it all. You *use* it to fuel your ambition and your desire to act.

Each day, each week, you have gained strategies, you have given your actor some room to grow, congratulate yourself and your efforts. You have used the tools of this workbook and your world has changed sometimes dramatically, sometimes only by inches, but you have moved. Now, as you finish this workbook, you might not feel 100 percent ready to go out and chase your dream full throttle. Don't worry, that's only drama. You only need to take one step at a time to reach a goal. Save all that PR stuff for the late-night talk show. Stay rooted in the "I remembers . . ." and stay on the course by continuing to read scripts and do acting practice.

You have put many days and hours into your recovery. You now have a traceable account of your work in your notebook. You can now see where you've come from and where you want to go. You have discovered a new fire to your acting. Continue onward and commit to doing the book over again when you need it.

I hope to see your name in lights someday. Trust yourself, trust the universe. I will leave you with my favorite quote from the musical *The Green Room*.

> *In the end, you do what you have to do. In the end,*
> *you do what you love. Because it's you in the end,*
> *that has to live with it!*
>
> —Chuck Pelletier

Tasks

1. *List five people on "the other side" who you can ask for help. Ask!* Don't be shy! They stand ready and willing to help you, but *won't* until you ask.

   Write their name and say, "Ruth Gordon, I need your courage to go on! I need you to help me through the rough times! I'm not getting any work. 'They' don't think I'm any good! Please help me," and listen. You'll hear something! You'll get a clue! You might hear a voice.

2. *Write short paragraphs of why you* still *want to act.* (Convince yourself to try again.)

   1. I have to prove that I can make money acting.
   2. So the world will see how brilliant I am.
   3. Because I'm good (no great at it).
   4. I love acting.
   5. Because I know there's a place for me on prime time.
   6. To prove all those lousy teachers who said I "can't" wrong.

3. *Counting courage: Write a short list of things that give you courage.*

1. Curious George. 2. My friend Amy. 3. Prayer. 4. Long walks. 5. The beach. 6. Bette Midler.

4. *Call your "acting buddy" and create a three-month "action plan" and check in once a week on your progress.* (Courses you'll take, new headshots, agent mailing.)

5. *Make a quick list of your current fears and angers in your notebook about your continued acting career.* ("I'm afraid I'll never get an agent." "I'm mad my friend booked a sitcom and not me!")

6. *Continued commitment.* Commit to continuing the course by signing the contract on the next page.

7. *Share this book.* Share this book with another actor. Remember actors love other actors.

Week 12: Check-in

1. How many days did you do your "I remembers . . ."? Have you considered doing them on an ongoing basis?
2. What script did you read? Have you started to see that the scripts you've read have giving you a great library of material to use for scenes and even small films?
3. Are you remembering to put images in your notebook? Have you seen any of your "images" come true yet? Seeing is believing.
4. Have you noticed any synchronicity yet? What was it? (Did any acting opportunities come your way?)
5. Any other issues come up for you? Have you been tempted to stop acting?

That's a wrap! Thank God. Take a bow. Hear the applause. You did *great!*

Epilogue

If I've only touched one heart and set it afire within the realms of desire, that would satisfy my wild notion. If I've only made one soul come from the darkness of living and into the awareness of what possibilities, what paradise dwells within their fiber, that would make me happy. Sometimes, I believe that I am a gypsy dancer frolicking in the streets playing a song on an invisible flute and asking people to follow their song. Fling open the windows, come outside and play in the ocean of life. If I've made one person become more of who God wanted them to be, I praise the sky for that magical gift. If I've lighted a path, if I've watched too many sunrises or sunsets admiring the show of the universe, let that be my reward. If I've been witness to the slow, long, gradual birth of an idea of the body of work coming into existence, I'll be justified in living. If I've healed and others noticed what I've done, that's divine. If I am run out of town, torn from limb to limb, tarred and feathered, or even my neck to the knife's edge, I'd still do it again. See, my friend, it *is* the fire that I am seeking. It is those dark nights of the soul when you think you can't that, I say, "Yes, you can. It's all within your grasp . . . Seize it!" If I've walked too many miles and my travels lead to a dark cul-de-sac without an exit, I know my soul finds a way out. See, I believe in the power of the invisible always invincible, probably silent, perhaps not. I believe we are all carry notes to sing and message to write and plays and movies to do. We all are healers with magic wands called the heart.

Congrats. You have completed the *Awakening the Actor Within* course. You have put many days, hours, and weeks into your recovery. You will require further a further commitment to continue to heal. The following is a contract for the next three months.

Actor's Contract

I, _____, am a recovered actor. I will continue to follow my acting path. I, _____ commit to daily "I remembers....," weekly script reading, and seeking support over the next three months.

I, _____, choose _____ as my "acting buddy" and commit to a weekly check in for the next three months.

While I may understand there are many acting paths to choose, I will commit to _____ _____ over the next three months.

I, _____, will begin my new commitment on_____.

_____
Signature

_____
Date

Recommended Reading

This is a list of books that are some of my favorites and the ones I consider the most helpful:

1. *The Artist's Way* by Julia Cameron
2. *The Vein of Gold* by Julia Cameron
3. *Ask and It Is Given* by Jerry and Esther Hicks
4. *Think and Grow Rich* by Napoleon Hill
5. *Creative Visualization* by Shakti Gawaiin
6. *How to Write a Movie in 21 Days* by Viki King
7. *You Can Heal Your Life* by Louise Hay
8. *The Psychic Pathway* by Sonia Choquette
9. *The Game of Life* by Florence Shovel Shinn
10. *Respect for Acting* by Uta Hagen
11. *Making It in Hollywood* by Scott Sedita
12. *Audition* by Michael Shurtleff
13. *Writing Down the Bones* by Natalie Goldberg
14. *Setting Free the Actor* by Ann Brebner

About the Author

Stephen Foster is an actor-writer originally from Fort Worth, Texas, currently living in Hollywood. His two-man show (with Scott Wilkerson) *Divanalysis: The Mechanics of Camp* was played as part of the summer series at the renowned Highway's Performance Art Space. Foster penned and starred in the comedy *Legends and Bridge,* which was extended three times at the Group Repertory Theater. *Legends* received rave reviews including critic's pick in the *Valley Scene,* spotlight in *Backstage West,* and was "recommended" by the *LA Weekly*. It garnered three ADA award nominations including best comedy and best play. Foster's (and Pelletier's) screenplay *Rainbow Sticker* was a finalist in several major contests, including the Hollywood Gateway Screenplay Contest, the Find the Funny Screenplay Contest, and the Page International Screenplay contest. As a stand-up comedian he's played in the Comedy Store, Improv, and Laugh Factory. Stephen cowrote the book to the hit musical *The Green Room: The College Musical*. He has appeared in commercials, and some of his favorite parts are Joanne in *Come Back to the Five and Dime*, Bomber in *Picnic*, Cupid in *Reindeer Monologues*, and Bette Davis in *Legends and Bridge*. He is the lead in the in the independent movie *Off Hollywood* and working on a TV pilot called *Exposed*.

Index

A

ABBA, 161
  "Dancing Queen," 131, 161
acting, 18, 20, 29-31, 39-40, 42, 45-49, 69, 98-100, 107-12, 115-17, 138, 145-46, 170-72, 179-83, 189, 195
  and writing, 34
acting practice, 24, 38-40, 47, 54, 71, 87, 92, 98, 104, 119, 126, 139, 153, 160-61, 180, 190
actors, 49-50, 54, 60-61, 91, 105-6, 108, 115, 117, 124, 144, 146-47, 160, 172, 178-80, 189-90, 192-93
  blocked, 71, 73, 93, 136
  inner, 75
actor's contract, 43
affirmations, 88, 125, 159
agents, 186
Amadeus, 63, 130
ambition, 170
anger, 83
Annie Hall, 107
artist date, 169-70
Artist's Way, The (Cameron), 24, 76
Ask and It Is Given (Hicks), 40
Attitudes and the Dance (Foster), 96, 136
auditions, 116-19, 150
awakening, 18, 37, 169

B

Beaches, 62
blocks, 19, 21, 28, 30-31, 46, 77, 81, 179-80
Brebner, Ann, 24
  Setting Free the Actor, 24
Burnett, Carol, 26
Byrnes, Rhonda, 40
  Secret, The, 40

C

Cameron, Julia, 22, 24, 60, 70, 76, 82, 87, 169
  Artist's Way, The, 24, 76
canvas state, 52
career, 158
Carpenter, Karen, 113, 131, 192
  "Ticket to Ride," 113, 131
Chaplin, Charlie, 87
character, 106-15, 131-33, 140-41, 146
character maps, 35
Collected Stories, 86
Color Purple, 62
Come Back to the Five and Dime, Jimmy Dean, Jimmy Dean, 56, 139, 151, 154
confidence, 170
costumes, 132-33
courage, 191, 194
Crawford, Joan, 165, 192

crazymakers. *See* dramaramas
creativity, 32, 73
Cukor, George, 165

D

"Dancing Queen" (ABBA), 131, 161
Davis, Bette, 193
definiate chief aim, 91
depression, 47
detachment, 169-70
DiCaprio, Leonardo, 171
director, 145
discouragement, 50-51
Divanalysis (Foster), 25, 59, 76
drag, 134
dramaramas, 82

E

Eight, The: The Reindeer Monologues, 129, 131, 133, 161
entrances, 130

F

failure, 94
Fame, 25
fear, 81
Field, Sally, 141
Foster, Clinton Stephen, 193
Foster, C. Stephen
  Attitudes and the Dance, 96, 136
  Divanalysis, 25, 59, 76
  Legends and Bridge, 55, 60, 147
  Pyramid Scheme, 126, 142
  role of Davis, 57, 59, 110, 141, 147

G

Game of Life and How to Play It, The (Shinn), 77
Garland, Judy, 85, 87, 165, 193
Gawaiin, Shakti, 88
Glass Menagerie, The (Williams), 105, 108
God, 29, 78, 92, 127-28, 136
Goldberg, Natalie, 24
  Writing Down the Bones, 24
Gordon, Ruth, 26-27, 87, 132, 176, 179, 193
Graham, Martha, 115, 182
Grease, 20, 61-63
Griffith, Patty, 131
  "Long Ride Home," 131
guilt, 81
Guthrie, Tyrone, 152
Gypsy, 83

H

Hagen, Uta, 86-87, 130
  Respect for Acting, 86, 130
Harold and Maude, 61-62
Hay, Louise, 88
healing, 45-47, 100, 153-54
Hicks, Jerry and Esther, 40
  Ask and It Is Given, 40
Hill, Napoleon, 87, 91, 125, 128, 193
  Think and Grow Rich, 125
hunger, 91

I

imagination, 70-71
interacting, 196

"I remembers . . . ," 35, 52, 98, 114, 125
isolation, 73-75
It Started with a Lie, 137

J

Jones, Wetzel, 55
Jordan, Leslie, 60, 67, 152, 161

K

Kanin, Garson, 26
King, Viki, 124

L

law of attraction, 40
"law of ten" game, 124
Legends and Bridge (Foster), 55, 60, 147
L'Engle, Madeleine, 62
  Wrinkle in Time, A, 62
Little Man Tate, 63
"Long Ride Home" (Griffith), 131

M

Maclaine, Shirley, 141
Madonna, 85, 87, 95, 124, 151
Marx, Groucho, 193
Men Don't Leave, 63
Midler, Bette, 87, 114
money, 123-25
music, 131

N

naysayers, 29
9/11 syndrome, 93
nonsense memory. *See* "I remembers . . ."

O

O'Donnell, Joseph, 58, 87
Off Hollywood, 56, 110, 131, 133, 141, 148, 155, 192
One Flew over the Cuckoo's Nest, 21
Ordinary People, 63

P

passion, 91
patience, 96-97
Pelletier, Chuck, 60-61, 76, 87, 161, 176, 192
Picnic, 115, 151, 154
Postcards from the Edge, 141
practice, 19, 39-40, 87
props, 140-41
Pyramid Scheme (Foster), 126

Q

quitting, 50-51

R

respect, 111
Respect for Acting (Hagen), 86, 130
responsibility, 111
Richard (classmate), 177
risk, 112, 129, 136, 172

Ritt, Martin, 60
roles, 162
Romeo and Juliet, 21
rules, 41-42

S

sacrifice, 95
scene work, 104
script, 105
script readings, 36-37, 106
Seabiscuit, 82
Secret, The (Byrnes), 40
self, 47, 67-68, 70
Setting Free the Actor (Brebner), 24
shadow artists, 22
shame, 81
Shinn, Florence Scovel, 77, 88
    Game of Life and How to Play It, The, 77
Sinatra, Nancy, 127
Six Dance Lessons, 86
"Song Remembers When By, The" (Yearwood), 131
spirit, 29, 114
Star Is Born, 61-62, 85
Steel Magnolias, 141
Stone, Clement, 193
Streep, Meryl, 165
support, 30, 72-73, 75
Surprise, Shawna, 177
Sybil, 70

T

talent, natural, 176, 178
Think and Grow Rich (Hill), 125
This Boy's Life, 63

"Ticket to Ride" (Carpenter), 113, 131
trust, 190

U

universe, 29, 77, 91, 123, 128, 136, 192

V

vein of gold, 53, 60-61, 63, 70, 201

W

waiting, 96-97
Welles, Orson, 193
Williams, Tennessee, 105
    Glass Menagerie, The, 105, 108
Williamson, Marianne, 29
willingness, 72, 136-37, 147
Wrinkle in Time, A (L'Engle), 62
Writing Down the Bones (Goldberg), 24

Y

Yearwood, Trisha, 131
    "Song Remembers When By, The," 131

CPSIA information can be obtained
at www.ICGtesting.com
Printed in the USA
BVHW08s2156020918
526276BV00002B/22/P